Night Office

Simon Jarvis
Night Office

ENITHARMON PRESS

First published in 2013
by Enitharmon Press
26B Caversham Road
London NW5 2DU

www.enitharmon.co.uk

Distributed in the UK by
Central Books
99 Wallis Road
London E9 5LN

Distributed in the USA and Canada
by Dufour Editions Inc.
PO Box 7, Chester Springs
PA 19425, USA

Copyright © Simon Jarvis 2013

ISBN : 978-1-907587-33-7

Enitharmon Press gratefully acknowledges the financial support of
Arts Council England through Grants for the Arts.

British Library Cataloguing-in-Publication Data.
A catalogue record for this book is available
from the British Library.

Designed in Albertina by Libanus Press
and printed in England by SRP

A book of *The Calendar*
To the Shade of V. F. Khodasevich

« Pendant toute cette période, il a fallu dissimuler ce que l'on pensait et, plus encore, ce que l'on faisait. Grâce à cette hypocrisie permanente, l'essence de la vie se révélait en moi, à savoir qu'elle est invisible. »

Every last person in this book is dead, –
including me. I'm talking to you, yes,
thanks to my poet; he, thanks to me; my head
shakes and reverberates, while, less and less,
the waves of sound diminish, and, instead,
a lasting silence fills me, and I rest.
Now in this blackness I begin to sing.
Invisible is every little thing :

all, all, invisible, but that, just there,
right at the far end of the long thin room,
there where the curtain is ajar, I stare
into the night, all night, as one for whom
all locomotion is impossible, and where
that thin gap stands, I watch when through the gloom
flake after flake of trembling distant snow
falls to the ground where I can never go.

They fall so calmly and so thickly; each
wavers yet drops directly to the ground.
They drift and cluster, like the purest speech
freed from all causes of dislike, whose sound
gathers, disperses, lets its easy reach
range freely through whatever thoughts are found
left in the air, available as breathing,
or in the open page whose quick conceiving

lets all surmises leave their prints and tracks
deep in its whiteness, where their pressures write.
Then, just as surely, these determined blacks
are filled by flake and flake, until the light
unthinking action of the snow conceals
every last record, and the gazer lacks
all means to know their having been. The night
welcomes and hides them : what each thinks or feels

is as obliterated as a name
drawn in the soft sand when repeated waves
delete at one stroke its uncertain fame,
leaving these empty flats. The corner where one shaves
is still invisible. The mirror in its frame
glimmers more darkly, where its pool just saves
the snow's dim lights into its silver, and
they fall more slowly over by the stand.

Dead, every one, and gone beneath the snow.
I search the past for them, but miss their faces.
They are where all the happy dead must go.
Only, in this dark room, I cannot know
their quietness, their sleep; my head replaces
each one precisely in his life, and so
they walk again this path from lungs to teeth,
escaping painfully from sweet relief.

Each bears his rhythm like an inner star :
each is walked through by some one line of stress
not chosen or invented, though they are
not accidental either, since they test,
for each imprinted pattern, where the bar
is lightly crossed, or halted at. My chest
rises and falls beneath my shirt, as each
treads slowly through me his peculiar speech,

sending me softly dumbnesses, impressions
left in the surface of my slow tongue, which
shifts shape a little each time. Dreams, depressions,
pass through my face from inside. In this rich,
yet monochrome, design, these curls, recessions,
vaults and returns speak, soundlessly, dip, pitch
their friendly spirit voices through my sight
and out into the European night.

Fixed to the chair, I feel their pressure pass,
each with his proper contour, and they grow,
diminishing the ornamental brass,
the wallpapers and carpets, since I know,
at every stress, each failed protracted task
pushed by each voice along its own and slow
life-prolonged expirations, and its worked
reasons of sound, its still unshirked

necessities of fear, desire and pain.
Tonight one little tune won't leave my head.
It rattles through again and then again,
sitting me upright by this sleepless bed.
I do not want the snow to turn to rain.
I search the adits of my empty head
to know its source; I turn my recollections
over and over in their wrong selections,

till I detect this pattering refrain.
Ten years ago I walked across the bridge
over the river in the freezing rain.
It would not turn to snow; the distant ridge
refused to whiten, while the ice again
greeted my neck, my foot just slipped, then slid
along the pavement, swerved, and then recovered,
right at that moment when there was discovered

just in the corner of my eye the vast cathedral,
too large for its believers, and just now
dwarfing small clumps of them in polyhedral
splendours and gestures. Its bright sharpened bow
went sailing through the night, to put down evil
wherever it might surface, so that how
this back of it disgorged the faithful, few
at this cold, minor, festival, and who

they were, could not be seen, but, from its gaps
immensities of music, and their wide
curves, flights and logics, rivets, knots and straps
let the machine preposterously ride
out into air, let open all its taps,
until the flood of harmony inside
burst on the courtyard, and its unheard shape
drew in my listening. I heard escape

the improvisor's long preliminary
repreparation for the full return
first of his theme, which he would twist or vary
in strong chromaticisms, whose each turn
hammered new wishfulness, so the unwary
or somnolescent churchgoer must learn
new cadences accompanying each loved tune
just in time finally to rhyme with June

December's treasures of the shortest day,
the snow-filled and the snow-transfigured city
recalling thought to what we could not say
had ever happened to us . . . Hope and pity
were swiftly summoned in the very way
the dominant collapsed, as though some witty
turn had revealed an unsuspected luck,
just waiting for us there. A passing truck

shook the whole road outside; at just that bar
the whole array roared up its triumph; then
its chords bashed out the tune, as to who are
in urgent need of help, or who are men
sleepwalking to a cliff – *Wach auf*, its far
and faint appeal calls through these ten years when
I think of it, as I do now, while snow
falls down and down to where I cannot go.

That tune's return was like a doctor's fist
beating and beating on the patient's heart.
Its blows rained down upon us, where they missed
their stony targets. Breaking on each part –
Adeste – dead men – *faithful souls* – then – this
refrain, with elephantine grandeur, starts,
flogging the dead horse of the past to life,
opening all breasts with its jagged knife.

That tune is not the one that I can hear.
A different line is running in my head.
It has no music; it is spoken, clear;
at any minute I will recollect
exactly what it is, and then its dear,
yet bitter, knowledge, will correct
this written memory, however sweet. –
V poslednij raz nam muzyka zvuchit!

'For the last time we can hear music'. Yes,
that was the sound of it, but were those words
just the correct ones, was what they profess
just the real thought I had, when those loud thirds
and sevenths brought me almost to confess,
to say 'descended into hell' (absurd)
and bring me to the bread and wine to eat? –
V poslednij raz vy molites' teper'.

'It is the last time you will pray.' Thus spoken
or as though whispered to me in the night
that line came to me like the unawoken
presentiment of total loss, foresight
whose truth I taste just here, in broken
breath, not now bread. It was the right
premonitory cadence, even though
I now mismingle it with Cochereau,

who wants to bring back life with heel and fist,
unelegiac or resuscitating
desperate harmonies – where what we miss
would be returned in total, thus belating
each moment of our having it, since this
adds to redemption one prosthesis hating
the lack of it, and that descanting anger
spoils in the music all its better, stranger,

lightness of luck, its free or easy yoke.
These lines of Russian lyric know just that.
They have no descant, lack that holy smoke.
They travel on without a sharp or flat.
There is no point, no terminating joke.
They move along until the moment at
which they stop moving, and the poem ends.
They make infinitesimal amends

for long stupidity and cruelty;
they heal with true intelligence a wound
whose false need closes, so that we can see
all its wrong urgency, its late and soon
merely released, abandoned and set free
into what I should hardly call a tune.
I sit here in the dark, and through my bones
each instant of me rocks with silent tones.

We were assembled on the station platform.
He told us not to leave, but rather wait
for his return, whose signs would take that form
we should know when we saw them. We should wait,
wait only, for that certain day; no storm,
however violent, should now create
an instant's doubt of his assured return.
It was magnificent; we felt that we should learn

in due course every needed detail, nor
should we at this time question him, but stand
receiving & accepting, and know more
at just those times and seasons when his hand
should by his agents from that further shore
send news, signs, tokens, which might still strike land
here in our clandestine assembly, tell
us of the last new happenings in hell.

Whether in Khabarovsk or in New York,
some word should come, some emissary find
one of our number : as the stooping hawk
finds out the field mouse, so his keen love's kind
and irresistible dexterity
should at each crossed road or each dubious fork
know how to reach that one of all our kind
who would with the correct celerity

alert the rest. The train began to leave.
The last I saw of him, through sparkling glass,
or what I could make out, where time can thieve
no particle of recollection, may not class
it with some set of likeness, nor bereave
me of one colour, one swift stroke or pass,
but still retains each single thought & gesture,
each hard-won glimpse & hardly-spoken texture,

was his retreating smile at once and frown :
where the cheek's stoicism bore its gloss
set by the brow's lines where they just turned down
but where the mouth's serenity took loss
for gain in knowledge; so without a sound
his lips formed one word which it was imposs-
ible to make out, though eye strain and ear
work its drums over so it might come near

that latest testament. A cloud of steam
took up his car, when with a soft sharp cry
the train receded, and its final gleam
was lost into the east; and just then I
saw two men standing there in what were cream
or white suits; they had seen us, and when I
turned away westward, they were at our side
almost at once, and so our own denied

perception of them leapt up from our faces
in panic when they wanted to confide
a secret to us, as from funds of graces
to let fall one slow drop, to come inside
each of our spirits, find its secret places
with salves or poisons, while they vainly tried
as if to calm us : "Don't look for him now.
He'll be back soon enough. You go back now

to where you come from : after all, this train
travels in both directions; whom it bears
away, it readily may bring again."
Then they were gone, and through the tables, chairs,
and other furnitures which in the rain
made up a wet refectory, the glares
of their departing suits could not be seen.
We sensed the working of some large machine

all whose preferred devices and desires
we could not know, but must attempt to guess.
It was as though the city's shining spires,
bisected by the interlinear stress
of all those energies detained in wires
were in concerted pointings none the less
to try to tell us what we were too lost
to know or even notice. So we crossed

back over then, eleven of us, and
we all went up into an upstairs room,
and sat there looking at each other, and
no one said anything : our empty tomb
of left bereftness, our dejected stand
here at this newest doubt as to by whom
we had just been abandoned, and our look
right at the next page of the wrecked best book.

There is no last time, but there is for me.
Each time this starts, I want to make it stop.
A stupid habit settles into me,
letting me wish to falter, fail and drop.
I want to pacify the quick unfree
leaps of my throat, to muffle at the top
each pain-fed melody, each real perception,
dispel each nerve into some long deception.

The Last Encounter – but no poem bears
that heading : all their hues and shades
leap at the first, whose recollection spares
colours, deleted from this poem, trades
its brilliants and its perfumes and its shares
quickly and glisteringly, or lights glades
richly from inside, so we wish to enter
and lose ourselves into its very centre.

So the electric candles, iridescing,
cast their imagined glances on a neck
whose lovely owner bends and dips, expressing
an unattainable perfection, decked
with some few ornaments, as though confessing
light's whole strong spectrum, where we can't inspect
an unmixed colour, but where all must mingle
round her whose beauty may alone stay single

in opera glasses or unconscious stares
from the police chief or the maestro, since
all eyes must fall on her whose light impairs
all other sources here, immortal glints
seducing into truth with silken snares
who will become the necessary prince
detained, imprisoned, tortured and beheaded
to serve that justice to which he was wedded,

while fair Sophia leaves the city, and
is never seen again, except in stories
told in some damp apartments. Stand
and turn the gas down. Little glories
of flame play round the vent. *Russkij Kharbin!*
you are deleted, like the Severn Tories
or like the works of Golokhvastov, and
your coteries, claques, guilds of poets, spleen

and ideals, and Pereleshin hearing
halfway to Rio the Parisian note,
its godforsaken whisper, in some clearing
like Hongbo Square where you could still see float
the pyramided roofs whose bulbs thrust, spearing
into the flat white of the cold sky. Throat,
revive that bench! Speak failing pages of *Rubezh*,
verse brought from Moscow or from Voronezh

along the Chinese Eastern Railway, holding
rhyme to its most exact requirement, set
just at each terminal, and there enfolding
whatever of indelible is met
between its clasps : so when the scolding
Young Guards come and destroy the church, you get
your bags, and, then, the Berlitz School and British
Council, one librarian; so skittish

monks know their Solovyov, Bely, Kuzmin :
each is chewed up into the heart, as glances
may leave more understanding than words mean
in some precisely calculated trances
you fall to *On The Path*, which, first (Kharbin,
in 1937) let some dances
of tooth and lip slip into permanent
black rescue from the all impermanent

condition of continuous deletion
as which life cannot not strike us today.
Cannot not strike me, since my deep accretion
of cherished wounds and grievances must play
into each moment, to each new secretion
of its decomposition, or I say
psalms of a measureless outside, a tic
I can't get rid of, a compulsion, click.

I by privations register its strict
command of disenchantment : I strip down
each needless colour, and I then inflict
on every thought this tune, I build this town
of chastened melody in air, delict
of stripes on print, until I with a frown
burn each vast poem and commit its ghost
to the most perishable folded host

of lobes and folds and trackless little gaps
in my head's one left organ. Then, this done,
I start again. I reconvene my maps,
placing thought's flag in every city : one
in Riga, one in Prag, another flaps
at Nice, at Cairo, as the whole undone
series of dead men marches : Biarritz,
where Blok fed cigarette ends to the crabs

or thought about Sophia, sometimes, drifting
in miserable consciousness of ending
drunk or indifferent on the sands whose shifting
could not be patterned, since their hot unending
slides of mere silica evade all sifting
and four feet fail before the never-ending
task of its comprehension, take the fag,
or die entangled in a plastic bag,

you're history, which means, you are not, shed
into the cold and meaningless Atlantic.
A proper name I speak inside my head
relieves me for one instant from this frantic
fury of disappearance, as, instead
of the police, I reconvoke some antic
precisions of a possible unknowing
at just what speed the whole damned thing is going

down to the pit and to prosperity.
Hell's cicerone, I yet may not remember
just where each special circle is; for me,
each more particular revenging ember
loses its name, and I can hardly see
whether in this perpetual November
this or that word burn fastest : where they stop
may be perdition's nadir or its top

pile of mere masonry, may be Biltmore.
This ozoned atmosphere, a boon to health,
demands a railroad for the many more
drawn to the heights of Asheville, and since wealth
must find a stone, these vasts of ashlar soar
unbrokenly, and limestone as by stealth
arrives from Indiana, and then surges
up from the elevation where it urges

its crestings, crockets, peaks and pinnacles,
its retrospectively invented France,
to mark the sky with steep stopped spiracles
nothing can breathe through : so the long advance
of turrets vainly offers to some cenacles
of lost bellettrists its whole heavy prance,
its hippopotamus mazurka, thumped
down in the backwoods where it just gets dumped

until it cannot be afforded, and
Edith must sell the village, and the butler
makes notes on spoiling draperies : all grand
writhings of oak rebuke the lazy sutler
and proud Karl Bitter's frieze must mutely stand
over the fireplace, while she sacks the cutler,
and, in the library, fifteen thousand books
await in vain a reader, or least looks

but from some one stuffed poet, more quite still
than an immense intarsia cut from pear
and walnut, suffering, where each can fill
his hours with gazing on the little stair
carved with a cartouche on the side or rill
of an imaginary stream, and, there,
in this hewn wilderness of woods, small gates
divide the upper storey into states

or principalities, each book-lined section,
an unread little world : so, here, the treasures
of Spanish emblemaries give direction
to fallen spirits, or the lively pleasures
of Dutch verse orreries detain reflection
into their fleet hexameters, whose measures
lie there awaiting a propitious sky
to start them walking. So the wearied eye

tormented with more ormolus and lacquers
rattles around the tree-deaths, flies from polish
to dark matched polish, gilt nutcrackers,
jets, ebonies, as though it would abolish
into these figurines of cash those backers
who ten years later would at once demolish
every last strut of it. Your look gasps out,
and falls, ubiquitous, on Olmsted : doubt

assails you whether these drenched gardens,
giving to park, to farm and forest, are
a hypertrophied film set, as there hardens
into your gaze the line, distinct and far,
of each picked obelisk, which quickly pardons
the unimpinged-upon blank gulf. A car
snails down towards the lodge, to say how giant
even combustion engines find these pliant

winds of the comfortably surfaced road,
and, as its tiny body inches down
along the shining grey, some dread-filled load
worsens inside my memory, some crown
of disappeasing poisons would implode
into my scalp, and now I may not drown
any least detail of it in forgetting,
but must instead rehearse the whole upsetting

bad recollection of worse truths. The rain
is falling quickly. Time to sell the house,
or, to reprieve it, with an equal gain.
Each plinth of wishing, each imported grouse,
records some fantasy, joy's death-mask : pain
must grimace from each bush the sky can douse
with a fine drizzle, till their wanton shapes
of boats or planes or horsemen, or what apes

in each trimmed case some object in the world
finds its eventual fate in Pammy's journal,
where the hot muffins and the soft unfurled
duvets of getaways, with each diurnal
sweet special extra, carefully are curled
into small narratives of this eternal
vacation, vacancy, time's mossed republic.
They had to open Biltmore to the public.

But that is not the painful name to which
my head is crawling, slowly, nor is that great park
far enough south : its every slope and ditch
still stands, preserved, so the electric ark
of silicon may grant some thoughtless niche
to each last ornament, and in that dark
pretended memory may kill it off.
From the next room I hear my neighbour cough.

I must abbreviate to an initial
each name I cannot bear; I must delay
to some reserved and distant hour official
notice of P. and X.; it is the way
in which I may thus in this interstitial
series of reminiscence start to say
what each did to the other : which I know,
but which seems now two thousand years ago.

"How many of us are there left here now?
Not much more than a hundred; say a score,
minus that one who proved to us just now
he would betray his mother." But before
he went on, P. just fixed us with a frown,
to let us know, if there were any more
who planned to squeal, their fate. "He's in the mud,
fixed upside down now in his field of blood."

For P. it seemed impossible to think
that he might ever do the same himself.
P., who, when questioned at the Polish brink,
affirmed three times that, as for P. himself,
he'd never known X., would not care to drink
with him or even meet him, and a health
to you, good officer, and, to that end,
here's fifty, given merely to commend

your stern exertions in the line of fire.
P. was our rock, whose necessary blindness
impressed his actions with that keen desire
still to enforce those cruelties for kindness
which I then shrank from : so he would require
those precise disciplines of just unkindness
which should at last secure, to us who yearned,
X., shining, modest, quick, resolved, returned.

Were some sent off to trash the traitor's flat?
New 'candidates' for the 'committee', say,
vetted and interviewed, to make sure that
they were 'completely trustworthy'? Infer
from questions what we were, as we all sat
there in that room upstairs to talk, confer,
plan, organize the counter-kingdom :
as if these six men and a dog between them

might by sufficiency of strong delusion
shake the strong state, or just a little shift it.
It was not like that – since our shared illusion
was not a certainty that we were gifted
with history's last trump, but was infusion
of trust from one known face to our face lifted
as recognizing in his eyes, cheeks, lips and skin
the lineaments of good inhabiting

a human countenance, and calling each
to the same broken radiance : as air
is curiously torn in tender speech,
yet mends as instantaneously, so, there,
his single interruption made this pleach
in the world's fabric, since exhaustless care
bent in each moment of his concentrations
to tune our sober raptures & elations

to their right office, and our several prayer
in wordless song convened its joint attentions
whose still involuntary stops prepare
these inexplicitable meant intentions
to the true key in which we had to share
the food out, like who uses and not mentions
the very notes of love and justice both
as though this task were no more work than sloth.

I mean that every part of what we were
can hardly now be named, because the names
proliferate impossibly, refer
each part to rubrics, each of which defames –
art, politics, religion – though these were
not then invented, still their later fames
usurp in retrospect each fair sweet action
into their one-tongued unrestrained redaction.

There also is philology of spirit.
Its task is negative : it must undo
the ten false names which wonders still inherit
when they're accumulated by all who
grant what is singular no kind of merit.
Then the most real and worldless may speak to
past masters who unconsciously connive
to kill it, news : I am alive.

I think it was in 1924
that I first saw the ruins. I was driving
along a clay plantation road, before
Natchez's Melrose and its gently rising
slopes, with their shimmering, their full pre-war
carpet of grass, and, inside, abiding
each welcome visitor, the atazere,
mirroring keepsakes as though panic fear

were not the meaning of each single item,
but this, as yet, some hundred miles off, when,
just there it was as though the tall trees lightened,
but gave way, rather, to what I just then
could see were twenty-four white columns, brightened
that very moment by the sun; so I again
stopped and got out. The pride of Bruinberg :
each bore bronze capitals, and all stones were

linked by an iron lacework, dwarfing all
the teeming vegetation which encroached
quickly and silently towards those tall
pillars, whose massive bulk as if reproached
all onlookers, as if denied its fall.
When I stopped gaping and at last approached,
the fat hot sky pushed down at me, the air
withdrew all breezes, and the dazzling glare

seemed to advert to some delicious evil :
unclassifiable, some recognition
was as though waiting here, some bad retrieval
of knowledge better not known, inanition
marked out in twenty-fours, like its coeval
dilapidated monument, ignition
of one quick spark in the unwatered forest,
my mind's thick readiness to burn. As Horace

wants Tivoli, so I can't stop reverting
to that white minute, like the pure dismissal
of agonizing hope, the sheer inverting
of worked improvement, and my neck hairs bristle
up in their silent mutiny, perverting
each resolution into interstitial
languours & tremors, losses & surmises,
slow murders of all futures & surprises.

The wind's sore moaning through majestic ranks
darkly rebukes this never castle's king;
enslaved to honour, whose stern funds and banks
stand longer than this ruinated thing.
The motor vehicle which slowly clanks
away into the dust would as though sing
in the forced notes of steel its single thought,
its triumph over this abandoned fort.

There are no longer ruins in the world.
Whatever bears the tin plaque or the label
has been disruinated and defused.
In each intolerably smooth, impearled
fire exit logo, is at once refused
the speaking pathos of this candid Babel,
that no rebuke may ever more be heard,
that no hard word may trouble the amused

stroller and chronicler of all this stuff.
When driving southwards on a summer night
the half light cannot pierce the glades; a rough
wind shakes at all these blossoms, as the white
darkened magnolias still rock and brush
the lawns and paths with glimmer; you turn right;
the road, a miracle of public care, disowned
by all who flit along it as their own

inflated bearers hum among the trees,
and never meet another living soul,
as though this world were like a painted screen
or coromandelled up until the whole
surface is covered with what's merely seen
so that a bird's tail intersects the bowl
of inky lustre with its brilliant arc
and where this cut curve breaks the perfect dark

I cannot not treat arbitrary lights
as though each breathed with its peculiar meaning :
I cannot not believe each floweret writes
some message I may never read, or, gleaning
from each brief reed a judgement which indicts
some unattended error, I hear keening
hover and murmur from each gleaming corner,
inviting me to where some hidden warmer

nest of significances might, concealed,
rest in a solid cloud or on a leaf
cunningly set apart and then revealed
as the revolving gaze turns from the chief
eye-catchers to those places where repealed
desire at last may settle in some wreath
or tuft of foliage, and, thus, absorbed,
may shed anxieties as it finds orbed

sepals and petals like thought's cure for thought,
life's kind mnemonic in this rapt forgetting,
where for three hours you lose the thing you sought
and find instead this respite from besetting
identifyings : so that what you ought
to be, recedes, for this one passage, letting
eyelight and daylight drift and intermingle
into this twilight where no tint stands single.

So in *Gezicht op Haarlem*, otherwise,
a seventeen-year-old onlooker finds
a farm illuminated from those skies
where the right cloud equivalent half-blinds
its greyer cousins, and his longing tries
just to locate his bliss, his shudder, binds
his sight to seek it through the coppices
huddled in thinnesses and scantnesses

or in the blank fields whose flat earths stretch out
their shades and shimmers, their expanse of straight
graded deflections of the sun, or doubt
whether he really felt it, if that state
had truly seized him, or if thought sketched out
instead the mere idea of it, a late
ripple or quiver of it in his brain
as furrows stipple till they turn again

and leave you in the mud, or trudging back
out to the gift shop from the high lit room
to seek one absent postcard, nurse your lack
out in the street, whose weathers come too soon
breaking the fresh air on your face and back
and he or you remember then bright gloom
of mixed lights coming in the real sky
exactly as though I need never die.

The incapacity for this is hell.
It is the extrajected soul, the self-
distributed self-sundering, whose shell
must leave its fragments in each street and shelf
before it tolerate persistence. Well,
I know one variant of that myself:
phenomenomaniacal desire
to fix each fleeting glory, nail down fire.

Translations are reburials. All saints
sacredly stolen bless those airs and waters
of their new native ground. So sweetest taints
of thefts arise in these unsung thought-daughters
whose counter-isometric music paints
in contra-rhythms from words' unsought quarters
to let verse break to the reverse of Babel:
mute tongues of fire in talk around the table.

Our house seemed filled then with a gale, a rushing:
our thirteen versions of 'The Raven' croaked
in idiophonations, as, in crushing
loss and blank leftness, there were somehow cloaked
new repertoires of sound, where all unblushing
bluffs would be called, all dry disdain be soaked
as if in new wine bursting from the skins
or sober water where it leaps and spins

so that between these cloven letters you
may hear your own tongue calling, and may speak
one to another, since this lack sets you
into those broken nations whose oblique
phonetic arsenals at work in you
hum, chatter, whistle, click with all antique
dedifferentiating mouth-improvements
to disinter tongues' mis-sepultured movements.

P. stood with the eleven at that place.
It was the third hour. His new-rung alarm
sounded across the streets, the marketplace :
just as the prophet had foretold, his charm,
this marked charisma, this unfailing face
captured with looks opponents who would harm
the still raw recollection of what X.
had said and done to us, his human text.

This story of the hundred languages
is a forecast of how the sacred people
will fracture into joys, refrains and anguishes
shared incommensurably, as no steeple
may mean identically to each. There languishes
in international gods what will unpeople
the universal cipher for one sound
heard in one tongue alone, as though it found

in the best adepts of that dialect
some singular correctness, some best grace
to prove equalities of idiolect
upon some one irreplicable face
where categorical commands are wrecked
yet born up too towards their proper place
since fairness which may not be abrogated
is given to each as though each were the stated

single recipient of all this luck :
as if the word were only flesh in Russian
or, pleased to spring up from contingent muck,
said revelations needed strong percussion
of stops or plosives, tongues, to come unstuck,
desired clanked canticles of lungs' pertussion :
so truths done down into the deep Voltaic
required to be revealed in Aramaic.

Incorporated words are names : their flesh
shines with unreasonable reasons, voiced
in ordinary noises whose fine mesh
is none the less eluded : I rejoice
in every name I come to love, depress-
ion's opposite, because their still revoiced
lists, fasts and festivals will still inspirit
what blank identity would chill, dispirit.

It is not difficult at all to think
that calling out a name should save your life.
Words may not, anyway, decline to blink,
remainderlessly to see reason : strife
of logos with its logic, pen with ink,
of loving husband with his wedded wife,
may not be stilled, except you wish to silence
life's living letter with its spirit's violence.

I can for now just manage the incipit.
I am not yet quite ready to be saved.
Where that name stands, I still cannot but clip it
to its initial, since the wrong I craved
still floods my body where I slip or sip it,
still holds for absolute the bright depraved
immediacies conjured up for that
worked life of spirit, rabbit from a hat.

So that I seek each needful deprivation
emancipating me from tyrant sensing;
I sit in silence at the freezing station
taking its nullity for the dispensing
freedom from spurious exhilaration
of ceaseless flying & remote recensing
of one wrong total, one wrong pile of gems,
one wrong anthology of precious stems,

or play through for the nineteenth time the moves
in Šefc-Petrosian, 1957.
Each slow step made by Black as though reproves
excessive haste, so that at move eleven
his Knight retreat to Knight One disapproves
the five year plans, and sets a piece of heaven
here in its shuttling, in its two steps back,
and, later, in those backwards leaps which Black

favours before advancing, as he shunts
almost unseen some pawns by square and square :
just as his heavy rooks shrink from the fronts,
his skirmishers sneak slowly up to where
they harden to an edifice which blunts
or rather chokes White's liberty, till there
is hardly room for any piece to lift
its wooden feet up from the board or shift

except into disaster, as dark Knights
retreat still further, to the corners, sides,
or saunter idly in that park which White's
move-bound paralysis gives up, provides
to Black, who seems to sleep, waive rights,
or lose the plot, because his ebbing tides
of scattered forces drift without a plan.
He seems to do just nothing, seems a man

content to move the paperclips from one
side of his table to the other, and
yet to refuse to end this : never done
with further nice refinements, as his hand
hovers, retreats, and leaves the move undone,
finds some more accurately indirect
stroke of delay, some method to reject
the imprecision of foreclosure, un-

delighted by loud voltas or cadenzas :
so when I follow once again this game
or convalesce thus from long influenzas
the clock winds down; the hour forgets to strike;
each least foot backwards makes its minutes cleansers
of the bright spirit; I remain the same,
yet other, since renewed by something like
these numbers leaving number : this fixed frame

of eight eights liberates both black and white
as though their fixity were some true grid
from which all colourings might leap in bright
change of felt air, or as this hominid
might in its left head know one everbright
unending real life, where each real thought did
take its own chance to effloresce, then drop
like rotten petals from this brief sweet top,

until move 80 must arrive, and White
may not not move, yet may not move : his fort
knows its first hectic mark of ending, right
where it falls sideways, as Black's single thought
pursued through blank forgetting, through each light
retreat, halt, idling, until White is caught
and all his unassailable redoubt
crumbles & founders, & the page give out,

as I do, should these voices ever rest,
which, in this cold night, through the heated room,
stir and commingle, a perpetual test
gathered towards me like the ones from whom
each good is crushed into the absent best,
each leaf unfit to decorate that tomb
which I may never visit, as I sit
& recollect the somersaults which wit

makes in a throat when the correct stress leaps
upwards from down, and the remembered measures
bear its rung surface to that note which keeps
salting with sentience its keenest pleasures,
or which then mortifies the wrong : these steeps
stand me up straight in thought, burn treasures
into that fund of ownerless delight
I draw from pennilessly every night

when from the lexicon of hueless roses
I may pluck names whose inks compose those sepals
shaped in the day whose broken light discloses
Helen's pale flank, and where her brief glance settles
the whole parterre's nomenclature uncloses
imaginary fragrances & petals
fixed in the mind's unaltering anthology
like floral abstracts of a true ontology :

as Aschermittwoch, 1955,
calls from its silver petals' backs those shadows
which haunt this grey rose when its all alive
fullness of shining leaves these *petits cadeaux*,
these polyglot descriptors, which arrive
like long dead thoughts to their Trouillards or Hadots,
gifts which are secretly dispersed across
the whole wrong history of perfect loss,

over against these cinerary blooms
the white bud breaks & breaks into its shower
of sharp illumination, as when rooms
are flooded in electric light, this hour
knows in Schneelicht or Fimbriata swoons
of unassimilable brightness flower
into these beds and arches of blank dazzle
or ranks sweet heads into their marching ghazal

whose armature of prickles can keep out
all rude intrusion, hedge with glossy fences
the neat enclosure where an unkind doubt
forgets corrosions, and its meant defences
drop by the brick wall where a little spout
refreshes visitors, as their lent senses
revel and rest inside the sole Ideal
reposing from deletion. It's the Real :

airs left in air to greet the wounded cheek,
pear and quince blossom in the sun-warmed garden;
walks taken there from day to week to week,
sundials recording what they may not pardon;
the lost, the poor, the sick, the lame, the weak
process in allegory past hearts they harden;
so names like perfumes reconvene the spirit
into its proper life, as I inherit

from all dead vocalists a thinking tongue,
from Madame Georges Bruant forgotten candours,
from Leuchtstern, blushes, from my failing lung
niche-notes extinguishable as those pandas
confined to three peaks, as I squealed and sung
my counter-Caliban to black Mirandas
itching to switch me off, and to the nation
donate five hundredweight of obsolete phonation.

Flesh rests in hope, but the resolved strong spirit
works also through this other sleepless night.
The dead are dead and buried : we inherit
their sepulchres, yet exit into light.
Speak freely, or be left in hell : inspirit
night's dark collectar to find out the right
eyelid or fingertip to be transfigured
or no saved face continue not disfigured.

Since the police knew perfectly where we
were to be found, it was just up to them
when they should come for us, or come for me.
Translation day increased our numbers : stem
to leaf and blossom from this stunted tree,
three thousand scintillations from one gem;
fear upon all of us from house to house
to break bread, read our work, or merely douse

ourselves in common terror. Not alone
dreads were communicated; property
disappeared too into the general loan
made from our debt by each to each. Unfree,
each binds the other to be unalone :
as, if the damned know solidarity,
it mimic the sodalities of blest
or borrow bonds & bounds from that meant best.

At around this time I received a visit,
from an admirer, he said, of my verse.
I knew at once it must be a policeman.
"I have some news to give you." "Oh! What is it?"
What followed was so perfectly deranged
I changed my first opinion for a worse :
no spook was capable of such exquisite
dullness and madness. "Machines have changed

the forces of poetical production.
We have been working on a new device" –
I let his plural pass – " – on a construction –
to harness every power of artifice
for the collective good. The introduction
of a small fitment to your typewriter
records each word, each stroke, each little nice
draft and correction of the gifted writer,

so that no fine thought ever can be lost.
These informations may then be transferred
by cable to a central office, passed
to a large archive where each point and word
will be retained forever. So, at last,
we have discovered what once seemed absurd :
a means to fill all possible defects
in central records, since this now perfects

our means for the collection of our data."
Infinitesimally he reclined
into the chair, like one who saved for later
all the best details : "The immortal mind!"
It was essential that I feign delight.
"My loud applauses to the bold creator
of this important boon!" I could not find
my keys inside my pocket in my fright;

I kept my grinned congratulations working
while I assessed my chances of escape
through a back window – since, for sure, no lurking
co-agent would be there : no man can ape
that special lunacy which blocks the working
of each sane facial muscle. He was mad :
his self-applauses overflowed all shirking
remnants of rationality. I had

to work out how to leave alive. But then
he rose. "We have already carried out
the work on your machine." He smiled again,
unconscious of the least small vexing doubt
that I were happy to be of those men
stored up forever. "I'll see myself out."
I dined out on this for a hundred years.
Since then I have learnt where to place my fears.

How may the sand resist the sounding ocean?
The pearl conceal itself from any hand?
How may still life decline this restless motion?
Or poisons lifted from the toxic land?
All with immediacies of false emotion
wish to be just, but just which wish will stand
is as inscrutable as which flesh star
hid in the brain will undo who you are.

A second nature of refused perception
settles upon the city like a mist.
A bare-faced veil, a disavowed deception
falls on that cheek which is not to be kissed.
A curtain to prevent the least reception
of air's sent breezes, which must not be missed.
I stare into this wall of aimless skitter
glared to distraction by its nameless glitter.

How long does it take perfectly to choke
all childish intimations of survival?
With just what thick variety of smoke
must we so fumigate the new arrival
that no small squeak improperly evoke
some unsolved question? There shall be no rival.
The lisping wish must silently be strangled,
hung from incautious clauses which it dangled.

This is the face of arbitrary power.
A motorway as single as a myth.
This is the face of nature; this new hour
fate's fate-made cruelty, kin's crypted kith.
I am disjected into sands, since our
prosthetic souls self-distribute to stiff
think-sticks & grits, earth's loaned excuse for it.
There is no reason, sunshine, just get used to it.

Why must I cleave to what is always falling?
How can a child not know its mother's face?
How may I not love those dead souls whose calling
alone makes legible a single place?
I am that very accident befalling
the apparatus for forgetting, trace
of fluff gummed up inside the cut-price sodden
saw that we must be absolutely modern.

The disestablished State! This Brobdingnag!
The National Mall : the national mausoleum!
You cannot walk in it without you gag
on nothing's ashes, since each big museum
rears up on pyramids : each über-flag
reminds you of the tortured perineum
of each outlaw this law's dead heart spat out
into that lawlessness it cannot live without.

Earth knows a port of Hell : the world's free hatreds
collect into continuous surveillance.
Privation's vast sarcophagus, one fated
parade of lack-love lenses, whose dumb valence
presses this diorama of unsated
pursuit of happiness into the palest
abashed sky fading like the thinnest screen
down to the ocean, to the lost machine.

Why should this shake me, but that each shocked stretch
of shrinking skin at once reviles and owns it?
Why must I shudder, why turn cold and retch
but cold law made the warm heart which disowns it?
All frenzied self-conceit would gladly fetch
itself to some sweet kingdom : what erodes it
is hard self-knowledge, when the soul's broke Lego
spells in pink shards its *In Arcadia Ego*.

Why shouldn't the policeman photograph
my *wife and kids* at all times, just in case?
Why not a curb, why not a tender graph
held at head office to prevent the wreck?
Since it is possible to store each laugh,
each cry, each fantasy, each click & speck
just for the purposes of common good,
why not have each cell speak the thing it should?

I must inevitably imitate
those good machines which are the friendly powers
sustaining each new luxury, each spate
of abstract freedoms which I burn like hours :
I 'have to switch off', must convert to fate
intolerable life, just 'shut down'; towers
at the horizon do not fall but glisten,
shining with each fact to which they can't listen.

So when the law stares from some human face
I cannot but receive it as demonic;
its calm smile, vengeful glare, a trace
of paralegal life, life's gone mnemonic;
justice as irony. I know my place.
Just as all modulations find their tonic
I grin in terror like the thinking statue
immovably awarded brickbats that you

withhold or rain down on its still quicksanded
place in the nineteenth circle. Hi there! It's
2093, and I'm still stranded
here in the gallery, become those bits
of smirking granite, yet I feel this branded
substratum of all joy and pain : this fits
invisibly into my lifeless face and gazing
so that no onlooker may see the blazing

world of incorporated pain which marches
each instant through top cavity. I shop,
I drink, wash, make calls, take on proteins, starches,
reformulate the programme statement, drop
my suits off at the cleaners, calculate the charges,
yet never move an inch : from foot to top
I feel incorrigibly, while my corpse
gets on with life for me, makes jokes, chats, gawps

into the middle distance with its eyes.
Dream on! This only means : not yet. Not yet
has the worst moment come (there's one, alright)
at which this sin, this this & this & this
meets you yourself as your beloved's right
clear irreversible refusal, set
into that helpless falling out of love
with no past, future, forward, back, above :

since the elusive central fear I felt
when I beheld in Washington the tops,
the faux-Phocion backdrop, felt life melt
down to that zero, as a hanged man drops
to satisfy his public, or a welt
spreads on the smacked face, so these doors, gift shops,
were the truth coming from the ancient state
to wake me from wrong life, and come too late.

I was the sick man lying at the gate,
the beautiful, when you commanded me
just to stand up : when what I took for fate
cast itself off. Then why should marvels be,
merely because this Theory of the Late
confines them to one island in a sea
bereft of wonder, certainly refused?
Why must we permanently disabuse

ourselves, if not that wonder is the stuff
of the last implement which hides that fact
under efficacy? It's not enough
that all the letter days be blotted black.
Each long-extinguished light must be twice snuffed
so everything that is the case be packed
in valid propositions and their lessons
available on tape in sixteen sessions :

Sarum Obliterated. Pica, fall
apart correctly : let your happy pye
resume its proper puttings-off, that all
unwanted octaves shall elude that eye
maiming their false brinks, and your pit's one tall
use of fixed rules constrain me so that I
send counter-collects of sung ruinations,
Eve's sanctoral of disobliviations.

These smashed saints sponsor me : their absent heads
are just that aperture of free reflection
through which I miss them. From abolished dreads
if it be false to drink this sweet refection,
more false still what would tuck up in their beds,
their first gone quarries, put beyond detection
each howling stump whose stone neck still denounces
rapacious greed which eats what it renounces.

Measure the white leaves! Some omitted days
may thus by inch and inch still be retrieved,
lost sees recovered from the perfect blaze
of temporary signage, since believed
hapax legomena find out the ways
to stick like insects in the undeceived
clear solids, these oblated obsolescences
exulting in their loops & blest excrescences.

One man must stand there in the wood and count.
His brisk collations make this unexplained
calendar-calendar, these years' amount
more luminous the more he just refrained
from all interpretation of each fount
codicologically self-contained
and hunted patiently to lost ancestral
sources like rodents to the keen-eyed kestrel

or consecrate a relegated shed
the better to explode each dead tradition
into its true survivals, shent and fed
with those real injuries whose clipped rendition
opens that wound without which you are dead
or leaves one chink in final inanition.
Sharp pen, swift hand, correct and overwrite me :
dark where gifts stand, collect me & delight me.

I settle down into interstices
whose soothing milk is blacker than the pitch
they salve the roads with : these short walks, or these
tiny processionals, from each gate which
denominates an air ramp, to its pleased
concession, kiosk, station, vent, slot, ditch
sending these shots into oblivious veins
here at the duty free, before their planes

burn up their fuels, retch, & leave the earth
which in our places we at once receive
as just stuff, just what happens : so each berth
cradles a slip of toxins, death's sweet seed,
reverse parthenogenesis, whose curse
milks me for everything I've got. Blind greed
panics through all its airlocks, till it seals
each last experience to its grooves and wheels.

Meanwhile, one more Martini. To this dark
and cabinned *vol de nuit*, the air lounge blares
its giant colonnades : for this stone park
white tiles, white panels, white floors, white space glares
with all nocturnal phosphorescence : stark
banners of freedom from, whose blank just stares
written invisibly. Each placard bears above it,
spelt in reflectors, this heart's lie : *you love it.*

I know this false street's opposite : I know
one faltering line along a ridge, where stones
press their made houses to the shape we grow
from each next weather held there, whose brief loans
of rain or radiance, mists or sleet or snow
leave incorrupt those reassembled bones
gathered by bones themselves to this lost plot,
this single field, this resurrected dot.

Resumed methexis, may the state's face know
an end to inconceivable privations!
May our participating gestures know
their musculatures, their retained elations!
May in correct dance all masks undergo
their heartfelt revels, their precise sublations!
So may the disestablished kingdom scatter
just tunes and duties to their proper matter.

This I believe to be the necessary
realm called for by a single real second
at which I could know for unnecessary
a myriad wrong devices I had reckoned
as life's own substance, as what could not vary,
since at that instant I was called or beckoned
by what is absolutely real : by bliss
unveiled & undefended as just this.

An air just brushed the canopy; three birds
sang their fixed signals; at the street's far end
a car passed through the ford; no words
disturbed the inner ear, nor would I lend
a single sign to anything referred
into my cortex, where the same sounds send
their impure noises to my set attention,
swoops, twists & washes to my best invention.

Sounds where the tongue may rest are stopped and furnished
tongue-shaped to bear the impress of that thinking
which unreflectively can tread these burnished
pathways of love's erosion, ever sinking,
more deeply truthful, as a queen with girlish
lightness first laughs & then with love's sweet linking
lets the first sound of bliss become her burden,
weighed through a life like life's unceasing guerdon,

nothing archaic, nothing burnt or broken,
but held fidelity of conscious wishing
kept in the same sound like a thought unspoken,
detained in lip-clicks, or a sunk line fishing
up from interiorities some woken
unformed recall of heaven, and then dishing
out on this salver of bisected breath
collected sentences of death to death.

Like cinnamon and aromatic balm
I give forth fragrance in the fields & streets;
I perfectly repeat : I walk in calm
unmeaning iterations, since defeats
of earnest striving let all kinds of harm
fade & dissolve, until the dead choir greets
with living counterpoint my rote-learned quoting,
restores the true intelligence of doting.

After the miracle we were detained.
Think, when I speak of miracles, you see them.
You may replace with any unexplained
appearance or experience, to free them,
this ailing word : you may in unrestrained
trust or credulity feel free to be them,
allowing me to walk you through this story
without erasing references to glory.

Detention follows on what is too strange.
Speech threatens to say something : to avert this
all fervent utterance must still be changed
into quiescent reasonings. Then convert this,
you bounding line, to the undisarranged
sequence of breaks! I do not now assert this
as singularly mine, but cleave my minenesses
into your elements and their tried finenesses.

That wonder which might not be controverted
brought an immediate release. No word
bearing such power could at this day be blurted,
nor, if it were, could it at all be heard :
since hearing with its listening tongue reverted,
at some uninstanceable hour, concurred
in that long sealing of its little gap,
the ear's blocked answer when you shut your trap.

Then narrative desiderates deletion
of nature's supernature : it may not
endure one orifice in its repletion,
nor may its surface know one air-stopped slot,
lest, by this interruption, sweet completion
or deaf elaboration of its plot
should by mistake itself be brought to wonder,
which at this date must signify some blunder.

He merely reaches, and the whole ground shakes.
Deep in Nebraska, one light fingertip
brushes a sensor, and this pasture quakes,
erupts in mountains, so the buildings skip
right down the valley, and the placid lakes
flood all the fields to leave there like a ship
one raft of turrets, and the drowned men trying
to clamber up the stair of dead and dying.

These are the signless wonders, whose kenosis
conceals, inters, erases & depletes
all notice of its wrong apotheosis
into mute secrecies whose song completes
its perfect parody of paradosis
tucking up baby bomb between its sheets
so law no longer is the end of violence
but both sleep sweetly in a stateless silence.

How may this not construct my saved interior?
How does the bomb not go off in my head?
As though this pitiless exterior
had no connection with an inner thread
woven too tightly to its hid ulterior
nameless bad act, the tissue where it led,
soul of the weapon, making safe each cell
with thought's best chemicals for writing well.

If only substrate of invisible
and wordless substance fall beneath device,
how can it then be in the least divisible,
or more serve kindness than the biting ice?
Can then the absolute be just this risible
scrap of thunk bone, salvation's inner lice?
I sit and stare into a total blank
unable to find anyone to thank.

Each unseen shadow on my optic pit
admits its Pashtun archetype : each wish
floating thus freely at the front of it
is branded with the image of a dish
detaining every signal. As I sit,
each mental mollusc, flower, tree, bird, fish,
cannot but be inverted misreflection
of total horror's blocked self-recollection.

I hoped till morning, when he broke my bones.
You make an end of me all day till night.
Cry like a swallow or a dove which moans :
weaken your eyes, turned upward to the light.
Hell not confides, nor does death know the tones
pulled from that brink, to tune your praises right :
the living, the living, plucks the proper string
as I loose music from each silent thing.

Armour of light is put on in the rain.
Only begin, & find this failing night
broken in reason's daylight once again.
Unfailing happiness may stand upright
as solid rocks resist the quick refrain
of what would melt them into air, or quite
annihilate, in them, each power of standing,
until no surface should escape this branding.

A walk along the shore; the pillow lavas
give way to foundered limestones, flat basaltics
dashed to the ocean where their stony fathers
crashed in commotions, as the peristaltic
gulp of earth's throat receives and still regathers
slumped breccias as the ground's base for its antic
leaps and eruptions. We walk past all these
steeps and long levels, brushed by gentle breeze.

Fair as the daughter of Jerusalem
and terrible as armies in array
the state bears buds but makes no use of them,
letting them drop like properties, so they
wither, nor may all springs induce from them
one sign of life, one edge unfurled to day,
but all these extras rot upon the pavement
in soundless wastage, like privated cadent

subtle doxologies which in your face
trip from the cheek across the speaking lip
raising each quite unformulated place
upon that wonder to a part or slip
of incommunicable truth or grace
which can't be made explicit, yet can clip
explicitation's vanities, shut down
ten universal grammars with one frown.

So this true faith of sceptical destructions
deletes deletions, till I may not doubt
this absolute reality : instructions
for how to put things off just fold : the drought
refreshes me with deserts, whose long fluxions
empty each word of what it is about :
about it and about it let my cry
self-blank to threnodies, all's each-known sky.

What if those hours of light be irremovably
divorced from me, as on this sleepless chair
I sit and stare into the vacant night?
No loss can possibly remove from me
my having undergone them, since at their
irrevocable stations, points of light
burn with an equal flame, one tended where
they never may return to human sight.

From this fixed vantage I may just conjecture
those torrents of involuntary colour
forced through the black streets on each lit reflector
breaking bright splinters in the dim or duller
walkways and paths : cash-canticle, hot lecture
driven or roaring up and down, each hummer
turns tropes and turnings and neglected glimmer
all night through each part of asleep or dimmer

quarters & regions of the city. So
this automotive mesonyktikon
flames without ceasing; while its bearers go
to their imperatives, these lamps go on,
passing from box to box their shining flow
so that no hour may rest bereft, put on
this fleeting garment, this swift dress of glitter
shed on the rain-clad stones until some fitter

redemption come to them. I cannot sleep.
Across my disenchanted retina
process those festivals I blanked : I keep
encountering, in floaters, perils met in a
look to the window, all the sharp & steep
drops of extinction which might let in a
single discounted argument of faith :
this negligible atom, shadow, wraith.

From each corona turns a jewelled wheel.
This long night office of the helpless traffic
repeats in blinks that ship, whose lights would heal
all night long, with rung splendours, these erratic
paths of those demons which we would repeal
with that incessant psalmody whose vatic
ranked bells & antiphons stare down the dark
like life's dead talisman, the sunk stone ark.

Immortal treasures of unsleeping fear!
Our whole bank's assets cannot stanch the flow
from cradle to the grave, so that, just here,
we hold continual song against the wound,
willing these long melismas to cohere
in sounding periapts when, late or soon,
we may no longer look past what we know
must make our destination, our last room.

I am incapable of letting drop
that jet of supplication which must leap
in spires & surges till it overtop
the lost staff, which then falls away, or peep
out of this interceding vessel, stop
when it break through, and then into the deep
founder & crash as the exhausted wave
makes down again into the vanished stave :

I am incapable, yet seek relief
from this inhuman duty, this renouncing,
in heart's parentheses, suspend belief
just as I cannot despite all denouncing
keep at each instant gripped between my teeth
perfected disenchantment, nor, announcing
with each next step some fresh advance to glory,
make each least phoneme one piece of its story :

because I am incapable, I flit
just when this inner ear should be attuned
to just those engine notes assailing it
as this long night's set lesson, but, marooned,
quite otherwise, in what drifts, while I sit,
across this undetainable or doomed
undisestablishable consciousness.
I cannot stop myself from wanting less,

or wanting something else, or wanting not
to think about it, and, by luck, just now,
I hear the first, the submarine C sharp,
the underwater octave, sunk coin, how
muffled in three partitions, in this dark,
sound unretractably the launch, depart
towards its top G, and let this black scow
out in the narrow cut, segmented, art

of water's waters' waters, and then float
its loping bass in 12/8 while the light
cantabile is rung upon it, dote
on tone, Lipatti's, past three walls, just sight
through the close tenements the next meant note,
a glimpse there where you may not yet alight
upon a sunlit jetty, nor yet cease
deliciously to glide along, surcease

of moorings, since these eddies cluster
in spurts and dashes through the grid of wet
marine streets bringing to collected muster
lanes & canals; so, floating, I forget
to notice each key flatten, but drink lustre
each time it sharpens, or just slip and let
what passes by me be both grand appearance
and at the same time spell the final clearance

which rounds this corner to the central stream :
now the light trembles, and its many crests
turn and illuminate in failing cream
this palest surface, while the tall behests
of the entire palatial avenue
reflect into the drink or make their theme
aquatic cortèges, when there burst on you
immensities of ocean : strike : sail through

to where this passage meets the Adriatic
or its lagoon, the stone set lake where sights
of small craft, scattered, counter Asiatic
marbles and porphyries, or send dim lights,
as evening deepens, like unhieratic
signals, distress flares, silvers, greys and whites,
pledges or tokens, from this metropole
to the last measures of its barcarolle.

When these conjectured voyages begin
it is not really that I cannot see
the dark in front of me, or blank the thin
strip where the curtain stops, where two or three
big flakes each instant drop down : I turn in,
yet stare out equally, as over me
the pale impressions of the falling snow
shed recollections. It's as though I go

two ways at once, immured in some romance,
yet able to look out, just as I wander
from room to room, or line to line; each glance
spies, through the verbal forest, springs, beyond the
line whose held segments lead their own set dance
so that each hemistich evokes one fonder
break, pause, refreshment, and the slumbering tale
wakes its next chapter up in time to fail

to reach an ending, yet I sit and rest
here at the water's edge, and let one idyll
detain, with violets, maces, unbrace best
all our forearmed intentions in this middle
earth of delay, of misdirections, lest
all fine surmise contract into one riddle
deleting Roland with his cavalcade
into this summary. This is unmade

since hippogriffs attend each shrinking comma
or take wing past a lonely peak and tower
where love's long gaze upon the fields looks from a
single window, and one darkening hour
brings saturnine reflections, verse whose summa
winds, climbs and arches in its circling power,
treads out its doctrine in melodious pairing
twinned to those tunes whose echo is unsparing

pursuit through thickets of each quick unclad
divine sequestered pallor : now my dogs
turn on me even here, since that sunclad
figure may not be known, so who sees, robs
himself and her of joy, as someone had
sieved to a cistern all the rain which drops
or cornered life into some secret tank,
some reservoir, or some collected bank,

and so, when I have read for long enough,
illimitable pilgrimages turn
into this ineliminable stuff,
impassive polyesters, and I burn
with self-unsleeping testimony, tough
metals and plastics for companions : learn
again precisely how I must be beaten
just by that tasty snack I would have eaten.

Do not negate thus these arpeggiated
tremors of sun across the lake : there may
in this stern dazzle shine the one belated
admitted luxury, where like glad day
rococo complexes of crenellated
turrets and ramparts renovate you; they
are hid now, under greys whose sober logic
monopolizes current theologic

recessional defences : yet one field,
of many, holds a house I know, whose dance
trips from the one edge of the oval, keeled
up to its ceiling, whose lost depths spell trance
into the giddy heart, and sight's string's reeled
past tumbling draperies and trumpets, glanced
up through descents to that abysmal high
triform solarity, the sunblind Eye

which stares the meadow-church into its marbles,
its scagliola pilasters, whose sweet mingling
polyphonously decorates or garbles
the flagellated spirit, or blinks, jingling
wrong iconographies whose painter-Schnabels
mix catachretically every tingling
shot nerve to where it fails into its seven-
fold bliss of bliss, its iced & thrice-lost heaven.

It is the antitype of Redhill Baptist.
Yet the same living waters do refresh
the heart's thick quicksand, when its happy lapses
burn through the grace-infected fresh-wrecked flesh
and dumb stones answer with their fonts and apses
in hymns, cantatas : then this natural mesh
is rent illuminated, and I dunk
my too protesting soul where Adam drunk

bursts into flowers of catholic reaction
as to the unanticipated future
drenched with all colour or lost names of action
since it unpicks the too concealed wrong suture
knitting prosthetic loss, this evil fraction,
into each single thought, and lets the future
speak from each obsolete grilled loge or fresco
its perfect supersessions of UNESCO :

peasant-cathedral which each working man
and woman pays for, till its wooden vault
float in these slender columns, and it stand
no whit more inessential than the salt
which savours bread. Now, brothers Zimmermann,
your scourges open skin's essential fault
into perpetual spring, this firmament
arched over each good which I ever meant!

The authors are in heaven; I sit here
and watch the snow fall in the silent street.
Each evening at a quarter to eleven
I think of those whom I shall never meet
ever again : from that hour until seven
they pass before me in their most complete
invisible variety, their train
of spoken diamonds, ever and again

subtending any voice which kindly lends
its element to mine, and lets me think
thoughts in the object, whose assistance mends
my leaky throat, until I eat and drink
obliviated airs, with what subtends
their gone true secrets : water, meat & ink
permit me just to take no care at all
nor ever venture to the stairs or hall

fixed to the failing notion of the last,
mixing this wish for what I may not save
with the desire to let this real past
resuscitate its losses, since I crave
insuperable plenitudes, unclassed,
or spring up equal from their coming grave
each self-resuscitated face, each name
whose single contour exits from the game

it sings the rule of, beats its broken bounds.
When the recovering addicted man
leaves off for some few days, and, in sad grounds,
wanders in pain, before he really can
think any thing except what just astounds
capacity to think, this simple ban
on every place in which he longs to sink,
making each thing the opposite of drink,

at some one second one day one lost thought
wakes up from the forgetting where it lay
discarded in the adits of the brain
and pain floods consciousness, as bitter day
strikes the hurt eyeball, which may not contain
intolerable light, nor hear one ought
upbraid his error, blocking that refrain,
still quite unable to devise a way

to silence it entirely, yet, some month
or some year later, when the same thought wakes,
unrediscoverable joy now hunts
through every damaged passage, where it slakes
unthought-of thirsts, harrows all hell, and blunts
each sharp self-mutilation, till it makes
the long sweet series of self-recollection
into the opposite of all deflection

and, when a little breath of air reminds him
of singular unnameables, fleet seasons
casting faint odours whose recall unbinds him
from self-set fetters, from self's self-sent treasons
into illimitable pasts which find him
determinable revolutions' reasons
to put one foot before its matching other,
its free, its equal mate, its walking brother :

so I stare out into the lightless dark,
expecting messages from light's withdrawal,
negation's melody, renouncer-lark
mounting and mounting with its idio-choral
corrective threnody, the flowerless park
stripped bare and sounding with its counter-floral
hymn of meant absence, its resolved strong line
watching and watching for the least small sign.

Signs come as pains : what cannot not mean, flowers
up from the lungs and thorax into blooms
coded with wishes in their times & hours
set as invisible in empty rooms
where unseen grace descends in mental showers
or hauls out bodies from their burnt lost tombs
until they stand, belated, dumb & freezing
caught in that light whose light cannot cease seizing

each sleeping face until it slowly waken,
each deadened thought until it come to life,
each soul which only thought itself forsaken,
each husband married to his loving wife,
each error finding truth by its mistaken
planets & voyages, its needful strife :
so each to each is pleached or pleated when
Greek thoughts speak Russian to all Englishmen

as though that hunted word might this day lose
its burden of resentments & just walk
across to Nizhnij Novgorod, wear shoes
bearing it off until it starts to talk
in Coptic and in Syriac, or use
all tongues as licit as a piece of chalk
broke off the downs and on a piece of paper
setting down travels of a line whose caper

takes it beyond where commentary might
discover all its sources in the sky :
an aerial philology of light
would be required before its ink be dry
to catch each vanished fricative, or write
all fleeting pneumatologies which I
let drop from time to time as I pass on
just breathing in and out as though my song

were just those inhalations and their ex-
corrections falling from my striding feet
upwards and outwards till there is no text
not resurrected into each so meet
redundant vocalise, as love needs sex
not to appropriate it, but to treat
sweet creatures as that language or that food
undiscommunicable from all good.

All friendship is imaginary : it
must be imagined, so it can be real.
Now, as I may do nothing more than sit,
almost unable to do more than feel
the absence of all sensings, I feel flit
from every spoke of the returning wheel
clamours and spells of the imagination
reanimating the surrendered nation

here in one bedroom, in one cell of error,
here in one dark squint on reserved lost action,
here in one shaken scene of love & terror,
one seat, one chantry, one struckthrough redaction,
one still dumbfounded catalepsy where a
gone trance still functions like a one-man faction
yet summoning each instant from earth's ends
the whole real host of its imagined friends.

They are retained, as though each flake of snow
which falls before me in continuous dark
were in some second world arrested, so
its single station in the air might mark
one inextinguishable point I know
thinks its own thoughts inside the snow's whole ark
floated above those floods of dissolution
whose first muds founder to this involution.

Somewhere I cannot see, a silver bell
chimes once across the room : it is the clock
whose sleepless business only is to tell
each little number. I hear tap or knock
those metals whose recurrences impel
some mental key to settle in a lock
and open on to prospects of delight
painted in ninety shades of black & white.

There a coast opens at whose further shore
three small boats wait; the clumps of people there
with nothing very much to do, do more
of it; in recollections I see where
sand's fretted empires may expand then soar
six or nine inches in the friendly air :
each silical confection sends one parcel
of ornaments & bastions, one castle

to be demolished by the levelling ocean.
Yet as each falls, as soon there spring again
new steeps & crenellations whose one notion
is to be ruinated well. Disdain
of all expense defies the long commotion
of crashing tides : these filigrees explain
in twenty million points their fixed refusal
to save their lives. Towers toppled for perusal

into the wash of salt that eats them cast
their streets and bridges, moats & granges down
as whose true depthless plenty may at last
pay up in water for the lost great town
where fathomless cathedrals buried fast
erase themselves without a single frown :
parks, palaces and pavements roll away
just as the sun dips to remove the day

and lights one leaping figure on the beach :
all work and pleasure skips up through one boy
whose feet grip down upon the earth then reach
with each held toe to the opposing joy
left on the other side : so he digs each
inverse canal to feed each failing toy
as though his curvets were themselves the arches
supporting mud imperiums : glee marches

right from the turrets to his flipped instep
which flexes, tenses, rings just as his finger
twiddles one sandy parapet in step
with its right-handed brother which would linger
one instant longer on the base, in rep-
ertory of granular redoubts : this singer
in pebble particles rips up his building
out of the strand until conjectured gilding

gleams from each tapered spire, and lets the sky
invade with low light scattered on the sea
which itself bounces, jumps and trips till I
seem to see there his each limb's will lift me
off of this chair, where I remain, to fly
danced in idea, or built with reasons : he
is my young father : these wild words break out
as from a child impervious to doubt

who does not yet know that the moon and sun
are rock and gas, but who has not forgotten
nor just suppressed that fact : he thinks with one
undifferentiated flesh-intention :
as uncreated he is still begotten
in pensive hydrogens which from all rotten
concerted vegetable scriptures mention
continuous love until the world is done.

Someone is coming for me, this I know.
The evidence collects inside my head.
As the spring waters may begin to flow
deep down inside the ice, each slight word said
trickles through stone within me, like the row
of necessary proofs : when I am dead
each leaf shall readily be reassambled
in the bound volume of my undissembled

panics & terrors, my corroded log
of nemesis-nomenclatures. Each night
I prop these lids up so my sleepless clog
of dates & times may etch its names in light
on to fear's retina, may think which dog
is proper to me, which peculiar kite
must lunch upon my entrails while I live
until I have no notion left to give

nor any information, but am sunk
into incessant & unvaried pain.
My cortex echoes with the same dull clunk,
skull's bony semantron, which once again
is struck and clouted, as the self-same chunk
of recollections starts : the room, the train,
the pale face staring with malicious pleasure
like hell's own parody of perfect leisure

into my pale one back. So I must watch
each least twitch that the curtain gives, each breath
pushing its film back from the window, notch
each hour in stress-points, or think crystal meth
equivalents from primers, since I botch
my vigil for the vigilante : death
must not surprise me, so I may not sleep.
First when the dawn breaks through the blackened deep

I may know rest and let a sweet surrender
drug my light eyelids, so I fall and drift
off to cool uplands where exhaustions tender
miraculous oblivions which sift
sharp pangs & terrors to the sink, then render
each back to me allegorized, or lift
my worst thoughts up transfigured till I see them
like inaccessible retreats, or flee them

to those cisalpine cantons whose hid peaks
for once escape clouds; yet their high pavilions
are just too distant to be clear : each speaks
in shepherd-emperors whose armed civilians
sing hymns from fields where chequered light's leaped freaks
sport, flit & glitter there; these equal millions
distribute needed bread with the champagne
to every citizen whose real pain

is salved & tended, & whose sorrows darken
just for one instant on the meadow, since
in this high kingdom every empress hearkens
to all her fellow-regents. I may rinse
in these long lakes whatever stain dishearten
my every gesture. To the east of Linz
there rise more ranges. Then I will wake up.
The milk, the tea, the table and the cup.

Before that happens there are still these hours
in which each little bead of fear must roll
from left to right across my finger : powers
of uncommanded repetitions toll
their silent tocsins. From its shelf there glowers
the godless totem, the blank clock. My soul
may not be switched off yet, however hard
I push its thoughts through by the line or yard.

These numbered instants may not recollect
their necessary opposites which wait
hidden in spring, where they, concealed, reject
production's sad supremacy; as, late,
I know one moment where I don't reflect
but just walk forward. It is light at eight;
the cool air blows across me from the field
as high clouds mass ship greys and then are keeled

on to their bright fronts, and their white breaks out
to let one least slip in the evening shine
like a fresh argument of hope or rout
of blocked bad troops : no part of this is mine,
yet I the more from that may still draw out
an unsurpassed remainder, tread my line
to where the river bends and I can see
in sudden stillness far away from me

the fen's grey dreadnought rise in speaking matter
of unintelligible tongues : yet known
not in their own thoughts, but to stay, then scatter
each alien lure, because unbroken stone
holds its unfeeling, cased against what chatter
cannot, from here, be seen beside it : lone
from these sunk ditches it does nothing, stands
in sheer inertia, on these ancient lands

the only house I see of any kind
and as I crawl towards it, it begins
to rise and grow, until its frozen mind
thaws into doors and windows, thins
each aggregated lump to its more fine
porch, plinth or turret, where collected sins
are interrupted in the course of lunch
meeting rebukes from weldon & soft clunch

and my mere stroll through abstract freedom darkens
just as the western sky is filled with light
and I move forward as if each step hearkens
to some deleted certainty of right
which rears up here still against what disheartens
any known second with the loss of sight
so that emphatically I progress here
towards release from nugatory fear :

it stands : it stands there : it does not withdraw :
the twelve tone canticle persists with news
of how least worked noise may revive that law
it systematically fractures, skews
through squeaks, explosions, grunts, when I hear soar
your voice, as mine, brush parapets, renew
just from this prayer, departing, in the aisle,
continuous arrivals whose first mile

is still to be delivered, whose last lamp
is day's first light, the true state's first real stamp :
tier after tier of blank arcading rises
up from the ground, yet each a little varies
reserved enrichments, so that each surprises
ascending gazes with its stony prairies
or then sends windows, and the eye surmises
eyes back here, one drawn breath, or glass canaries

piping invisibly from through the rock
whose tripartite stepped setting climbs and clambers
to trefoil-headed arches which unblock
here again windows framed in quarried ambers
driving my neck back as the sight would lock
attention to collected liquidambars
in nook-shafts' shaft-rings and sunk quatrefoils
in circles in the spandrels whose high coils

end in a corbel table and late battlements :
the angle-turrets echo this : the apsed
chapel ignores the transept : its flat dents
go three steps higher, as the now collapsed
north tower would have done too, where expense
carries the shafts up in the middle, thought
impossible if not in England : sport
of the luxuriant and still unlapsed

invention, blenching at no prohibition,
until the westwork is completed, porch
with puzzling galilee whose dogtoothed mission
binds its arcades in interlockings, scorched
and taught, so that this rhythmed exhibition
both fortifies this with a chaste debauch
of rhyming arches, bars you and invites you,
a fiat which both shakes you and delights you,

until I tremble through the threshold, stumbling
half-re-fixated and half-still-refusing,
dragging my brain through as the feet go grumbling
where the inexorable still accusing
uncomfortably narrow, high, long, nave sends tumbling
marches of repetitions through this bruising
walk to the evermore deleted altar
whose central distributions may not falter

until I face the crux, the dark carnation
fixed where each line's construction meets the other
impossibility of incarnation
opposing and exhausting its loved brother
so that the dead heart of the unsold nation
must here in agony recall its mother
and at this blackest point one point of light
drops in my disbelieving face as bright

infinitesimal lit interruption
at which I cannot but look up to find
mere light and air break eightfold in eruption
downwards diagonally from this blind
triforium as if its incorruption
could find an answer in the self-slumped mind
which stirs itself, renews, awakens, set
here at this instant upright : Now you let

me go, and I stand up, walking unsteadily,
on and back out, as if this light might break
in pieces on the floor, or totter, readily,
back down the pavement, amble, haver, make
of each uncertain step a note unreadily
sung on the other, or just let each take
its own time. The inalterable heart.
The last lamps are extinguished : I depart.

These seconds may not recollect all this.
The words recall it for me : they collect
in their unthinking swashes what I miss
from each part of my head. So I reflect
even in this fixed bedroom. What's amiss
restores itself in squid parts : I select
in this way all the pieces of a poem
placing each part with negligences *v moem*

serdtsem, this printed one, till it become
its own long catalogue of objects : pens,
pencils, papers, hoarded like the dumb
relics of sanctity, awake! Each sends
just at the necessary time for some
unforeseen possibility which mends
a lost rhyme with a photograph, a gap
in thinking's tesselation with some trap

or glossary, reserved and filed, then stacked
against that instant when one lost digression
calls it to service where a word is lacked
or stress retrieving a dismissed impression
back to its sounding life. Lost loss is tracked,
not to a plenitude, but to compression
of thought's real odour in a folded pattern
flattened to three dimensions on this platen,

this labyrinth of infinite evasions
until I am exhausted. I recall
the very thing which long delay's persuasions
had helped me not to. Now at last it all
comes down on me. These delicate abrasions
sever the thread. Now everything can fall.
No music any longer can deceive me.
The moment when you knew you had to leave me.

"I left the flat. I saw him standing there
in the wide open window. He was clinging
with both hands to the frame. As he stood there,
dressed in his striped pyjamas, it came ringing
through me as what I knew I could not bear :
he stood like someone crucified. I left.
He then remained, lit up in all bereft
fixation. In the next street, I heard singing."

There is one instant in each day or night
which nothing may replenish or redeem.
It sits immovably, a hole in light,
refusing every ornament or theme.
It may not be evaded; its fixed right
is payment on the nail; no tune or dream
may work it downwards, since it never blinks,
but stares back blankly in the thing which thinks.

To me this instant is a faithful friend.
It is like an anticipated wound
dreaded each moment, so that, in the end,
when pain arrives, it never is too soon.
Perfect reality has come again
into my waiting substrate, as the moon
shines irrespective of my thoughts or wishes
illuminating all the sink's stacked dishes.

At such a punctual annihilation
I reach incontinently for that single
image disowning human obligation :
I wish to see that city which won't mingle
its pure diagonals with long duration :
I want the pyramid, want nails to tingle
with all inhuman cash, want concrete nero :
Chicago Landscape #190.

I misappropriate this picture when
I want to disappear. The slice of light
which broadens from the left to the top right
acclerates its props, which, rising, then
break into wires and boxes; outside, bright
pairs of white pillars with their thick struts open
to nothing, since they lack their born street, stand
bridgeless & therefore monumental, and

rhythm this empire either to be made
or even now to be corroding, as
there at the right a flexing curve puts shade
down on the vast lot, when it rips its mass
out of the photograph; the eye must trade
back to the triangle of black, and pass
into its almost indiscriminable
dark charcoals, where, yet, ineliminable

lines of that bridge's underwork are seen;
and, since apparent seamless night has faltered
into these less black girders, what is seen
seems to confide more detail : all is altered
so that some kind of tractor or machine
is minuscule at left, the staffless halted
capacity for almost nothing; then,
right in the furthest pillar-panel, when

my brain starts waking up like this, a tower,
a water-tower, and there is the horizon,
the least important line here, since all our
blanked gazing flies into the spiegeleisen
whose wordless massifs set their stony power
in lines whose rhyming with the lighter greisen
leaves this quite distant unimportant straggle
of trees and little huts to drift and taggle

unevenly and hard to see behind
the motorcades of architecture tensed
to shock and ravish the resistless mind :
yet, after this, the little scratch of dense
inhabited irrelevance aligned
there at the wobbling edge of the immense
puts up two squat spires like an ancient joke,
a weakness, smutch, a fault, a false step, smoke.

So I have found my failings even here.
The most majestical republic leaves
me stuck to some twig or brick, since lovely fear
is lovely for one hour, but then deceives
love and all blackens to this hard & sheer
loss, and the tip it drops when it bereaves
is these few bits of habitable clutter,
these plants, spires, chimneys, and their clapped-out mutter,

but take my consolation from the fact
(or my conjecture) that this faltering line
was the foundation of the picture, tracked
first so that strident triumphs might align
their route, around what they should else have lacked :
this lip or wound where earth has left one fine
open edge vulnerable to the sky.
This may consist of nothing, yet defy

our empty gaze, as, when his teacher said
he had to 'find his voice', he found, instead,
a banquet camera with a broken lens
and took it out into the fields to see
what he could see with it, and set it up
where in the slightest breeze its tripod shook
so that he had to know that instant when
calm intermittence might allow him to

expose his film one second to the light
leaving the single band where ground meets air
to be cropped out with knives so that the right
long strip of the horizon would be there
letting each post or pole score through the bright
wash at the back of them as though this care
recording each implacably must mean
that every little twist and quiver seen

bore its own necessary sense : so that
his spectrographs of these horizons make
a natural scansion of the wide and flat
edge of bereftness, yet their cut back shape
deletes to thin truth all the once too fat
scenes of America, just runs a tape
into the listless brink whose distant shore
is Midwest Landscape #24.

In theory I should like to drive a car
through every inch of it, & each motel
should let its lettering eclipse a star
invisible above, & each hotel,
each pool, each parking lot, each lobby, bar
should with reiterated speech go tell
numbers by numbers of appealing freedoms
refusing to divulge their needed reasons.

This is the kind of thing I think I want.
Impersonality in person, sent
in free parabolas, a blank descant
on no tune under them, so that each front
ascends from measure, and the pale or faint
glitter of phosphor is a lonely tint
delighting lovelessly in all that can't
confine or even know it, so it won't

    ask for the check or point out that the cloud
is made of water as it floats and spools across
my black sedan in little. Disallowed :
this makes the charm of each recorded loss
whose passing I may not lament, aloud.
I watch each helpless image run across
the hood, then disappear into the night.
Goodbye from now to being in the right,

farewell to lofty projects. Literature
became repulsive to me long before
I died; and so the topics of my pure
deliria recalled both less and more
than some minute particular : each sure
moment or colour lost its clear allure
because "there are no longer any sounds.
Can it be you don't hear this?" What resounds

is information, and its instant travels
on the erased earth's surface, where I rest.
The first known minute when a life unravels :
pain's matchless instance, pain's unholy test.
The long car leaving on the graded gravels;
a failing in your face; flight, or arrest;
the morning when you cannot go to work,
pinned to the bed. The broken cheek must shirk,

today, each smallest meeting, flinch or shrink.
Verse is the catalogue of thought corrosions.
It is not that I wish or even think
to bring an end to these required explosions;
I only wish to so deploy this ink
that each be partnered with the right implosions
compacting passion at that soldered letter
fixed to the spirit which it best can fetter.

I am the instigator : I set fire,
not douse it, when I clip each needless word;
in me those sounds which cannot be for hire
settle in each head where they first were heard.
I from the middle of a quenchless pyre
burn irreversibly, as though referred
from flame to flame in order to preserve
combusting life whose perishable swerve

fails always, never to be once extinguished.
This sort of thing I do when it its raining;
on holiday; or, when there is a strike.
Each several bell may be at once distinguished
from each, as, when their notes sound, unalike,
from air's shook sheet there tears this unrelinquished
distinct rung minute. Here I am, entraining.
I bring, to this, each sharp thought of dislike.

Meeting with Bely on the stairs. He lacked
a face. Nothing was said. We merely looked
each at the other, at the coming fact :
total oblivion of each line and book
susceptible of being read. His back
retreated up the staircase, while I took
the other way, and reached my destination,
there to find Lunacharsky's invitation.

The six of us advanced across the river.
One had a permit, and to this dark slit
the guard admitted us, the one met giver
of recognitions. When we entered it
we knew collectively a single shiver
in silence, snow and night. The only lit
part of it flickered in the basement, where
a garage dimly glimmered; then, a stair;

we climbed it in the dark, and, at each turn,
a sentry stood in silence; then, at last,
a landing, and a heavy door : to learn
what lies behind this, only, please, advance :
here : the white corridor : where there would burn
a brighter light than ever in the past
and a red strip of carpet drove our steps
down to the mirror at the end; then, left

to Lunacharsky's quarters. Crimson satin
covered the seating, while the blacks and lacquers,
palatial meubles, sang their counter-mattin,
since vesperously darkening their backers,
this funerary furniture not sat in
to which the personnel formed floats and trackers :
interior directly from the 'eighties
to show us how unwithering the state is.

But Lunacharsky was not there alone.
A certain Rukavishnikov was with him.
This remained seated, as we all were shown
to our soft stations, as if this would give him
some evident advantage, some high tone;
he barely – dipped – his head, seemed hardly living.
As Lunacharsky readily explained
the new conditions which henceforth obtained

and which all loyal artists, mimes and writers
would necessarily observe, his waxwork, friend,
in a green service jacket, still invites us,
with his chill simper, closely to attend
to his clear merits, as to what unites us
in strong assistances to one great end :
Gesamtkunstwerke in three hundred acts
delivering in top-class verse the facts

to local branches. Lunacharsky finished.
We were acutely mortified. It was
impossible to move; each face, diminished,
fell as we sat, immobile. High jet gloss
looked hard at us. Our shame stood undiminished.
The interview seemed over; but there was
more still to come, since Rukavishnikov,
after this pause, a stammer, started off

in exegesis and amplification
of all that Lunacharsky had just said.
We were to know the noblest of all stations.
We should take meals together. Each, clothed, fed,
should taste exquisite joys and gratulations
of our co-operative art work, tread
those floors of marble, glass and aluminium
which would be our collective condominium.

We rose. We each shook Lunacharsky's hand.
We left in silence, passing by the place
where Rukavishnikov was seated, and
without a glance at him, each fallen face
was carried to the corridor; each hand
tumbled down slack; in each's joint disgrace
we, at the entrance, met a splendid sleigh,
draped in rich cloth and bearskin. "By the way,

just whose ride home is that?" We soon heard back.
"It's Comrade Rukavishnikov's." We walked
down where the bridge's black refusals balked
all possible reflection, while fresh lack
stared simply back at each of us. None talked.
I then first knew the unreceding track
I tread still, in this room, as I stare out
into a night devoid of any doubt.

I require nothing, but what comes is this :
more lonely products fill the streets and rooms
until the whole supply of silence is
exhausted, as each word should bear thick glooms
of cash-packed imprecisions, so it miss
each proper object, and prepare lit tombs
for all experience, which is obsolete.
So my tongue's route march on its hands and feet

need not imply that more of this is needed.
Less would be better, but the blanked word's field
calls for that harrow by which it is seeded
with cuts, abrasions, till some furrow yield
that seen leaf which had otherwise receded
quite from the world; until it come, I wield
these thousands' thousands like a penny whistle
to make your neck hairs start, turn, wake and bristle.

You are the only one for whom I write.
Even in this bocage of verse, your mind
has tracked me down, so that this room, this night
are not so hidden but that you may find
my last intention, hope, thought, wish or fright
inalterably buried in a line
and then unpacked, quite other, yet the same,
illuminated with your secret name.

Your history is what is unforeseen
by any instant of this verse; your thoughts
think by themselves, until the choking screen
melts to your quiddity; your vessels, ports,
your trains, your flights & systems are not seen;
your coteries, your papers & your courts
each are from this lost box completely hidden
as just that note by which it may be chidden :

that note which every line I write must seek,
must fail to capture, or detain one second,
since its economy, its true antique
or perfect modernism can't be reckoned
in any numbers I possess : I speak
to let that note sound, as my each line lessened,
by dozens, imbecilities which block you,
as though these thick clacks might at last unblock you

to melody which may not be contained
in any metre, and which does not need
these figured motors, since the still refrain
of sound's returning contour lets it lead
its unadorned material, its lane
of unassimilable twists, & speed
in undeluded beauty like thought's texture
left unintentionally in its gesture.

Make then these cells your sump : rip, tear, & wrap
their long recurrences, until you score
one fair line through them, so the whole framed trap
become that substrate where you merely draw
in purity of heart that ceaseless gap
which to this plenitude may still restore
loss like the secret of life's else crossed glimmer.
So may your new line tremble, speak and shimmer,

as unanticipatable as Lulu's
still vibraphone whose scale goes up electric
through the interiors of Honolulu's
ekstatic skyscrapers, where their selected
zeniths caress the heavens, or call Sulu's
island flotilla back, as each eclectic
pattern or graph at once emancipated
from metre's fetters and its too belated

rivets of rhyme, shall work loose, and ascend!
Here in this silence I may still recall
its single timbre : when the strings descend
in these chromatic slumps, their long song's fall
as though a leaf were withered to its end
right in my hearing, then there lifts from all
forlorn bassoons and trombones this clear tone :
an unassimilable vibraphone

whose note's pure panic, yet is also lust,
is the same bell of exit and despair
sounded on entry, as its clear thought just
indifferently as angels drops all care
for heart's entanglements, in perfect trust
to the black ziggurat of debonair
negations, cruelties, and blank rejections
from which it coolly orders its selections.

It is that efficacious opposite
which counter-masters magic : it floats up
in automatic incantations, fit,
deleting supernature, to bind up
all signs and signals in a little bit
of lunar metals, the unmeant sent cup
of hopeless treasures. Heaven help us.
Dejection's empire, plus prosthetic helpers –

not that I'd ever turn the morphine down –
since these electric tintinabulations
may be the final chime *seit je* set down
from the first military adaptations
of tinkling bronzes striking terror sounds
to present cruelties & mutilations
whose strong fear then we bring to come and dwell
inside the illocutionary bell.

Must I therefore hear further from each light
and silver signal in the nave or choir
its undersong of unremitted fright
as the home hearth contains a martial pyre
or murders sponsor every gaudy night
down to the least flounce which I must admire?
Not only this : the resurrected letter
brings back that spirit which can make it better

or coppers smelted down to make artillery
can just melt backwards, so the little nola,
the squills and cymbals, offer one ancillary
harmonic which eludes Savonarola
and goes unheard, as the unique fritillary
thrives in one valley, or survives in polar
spots of austerity, whose paradise
may not be disinvented, but braves ice

like that lost thought which lives and thinks on kept
deep in a dozen libraries at once.
Trust of this held me when I blithely stepped
forward insouciantly as who hunts
in lifelong patience, comes like one who slept
the whole pursuit long, till he then confronts
retrieved concealed delight in its true courts
sequestered from all merely formal oughts

for real deontology : this scent
perfumes a whole life when the proper place
inside that life is found, as it were sent
and chanced on, both, or, when my lover's face
I meet by accident upon the street
seems to confirm that happiness is meant,
is perfect amerimnia, complete
insouciant justice or methectic grace.

Lexiques du désert! you are just that map
of the large territory which from my bed
extends to door and window : each sharp trap
which natural demons place there, goes unsaid
until your treasury sets just that gap
at the one sentient corner of my head
and stops with necessary apotaxes
each opportunity for parapraxes :

lusus, sed non naturae, I may stumble
from bed to chair, and back again, until
deskbound processionals just vault and tremble,
cavort renunciations, and I fill
my heart's reverse sclerosis, clear its jumble
out for refreshment from that unchecked rill
of hesychastic disaffiliation
from each wrong loyalty, each raging nation.

I lack unfeeling armour : you may wound
me at a dozen points, since no thick skin
makes it impossible to bless me. Soon
my cicatrices will again begin
their failed self-sealing, and acedic noon
bring its ennuis, which open & let in
that irremediable lack which saves me
like the true lover who requires and craves me.

His nature bends all nature to his work.
His faith permits it to lie down and shirk.
His nature sends all nature to its work.
His faith permits it just for once to shirk.
His nature's nature has no need to shirk.
His faith performs with pleasure all its work.
Faith's nature, nature's faith, may repetition
believe and be faith's natural disposition!

I will not say that I am a device.
The semicircle where my heavy lyre
gives up its hard notes, looks out over ice;
tall poplars to the right; one may admire
how in the distance that dome can entice
from its squat cupola to the entire
warehouse of print on which the state has fed
its house of authorships, its empty head.

I am illuminated by the sixteen watts
sent from above me in a plaster sky.
From that high bulb there fall the shining plots
of light on bed, and chair, and table; I
still sit here thinking, but I still do not
know where to put my hands; time moves on by
the silent blossoming of palms of frost
there on the glass; each minute that is lost

sounds its tin inch inside my pocket, and
a silent melody begins in me
walking its rhythm through my feet and hands
until advancing amphibrachs set free
some subterranean fire whose column stands
up in my tongue till I cannot not be
wholly unconscious of the stucco ceiling,
wrenched by one calque to legislative feeling,

and the cold city facing to the west
seems to repair its injuries and lesions
just as this mouth is wounded with the rest
or be itself a wound whose vent freed reasons
just by this interruption, or redressed
by this suspension of my abstract freedoms
the catatonic claques of information
sounding and sounding through the surplussed nation,

and I may be permitted to recall
one still night in the lost late summer garden
where the cool intimations of a fall
brush my face gently, as if some vain pardon
were kept for me by the espaliered wall
or some one memory refuse to harden
into that edifice of fixed oblivion
we build each morning like death's fresh dominion,

so that those promenades whose avenues
disclose each at one end some little plinth,
urn, god, or beast, may please, or, may accuse,
or place some lilac, rose or hyacinth
as though its colours were the longed-for news
known in the last fold of the labyrinth
and which might, by that detail which unsettles,
return me to epiphanies of petals.

The whole day builds its heat towards this cooler,
yet still intensely warm, transfigured night :
it is as though the earth should need no ruler
stronger than air or water, since the flight
of each delicious breath of air would spool a
long strip of cold relief across the tight
hot inches of my face : it is as though
life need not worry, or might wander so

through each late hour of daylight that its walk
should be itself the necessary figure
constraining harms with nothing more than talk
or sweet fruits grow there, not without a digger,
but without withering on what would balk
their pungent qualities to signs, refigure
the plum's one texture to a mark of some
distinction or recursion over dumb

stuff : in the tree of roses on the wall
two hundred convolutes of interwrappings
pleat white on white repeatedly till all
the house behind them is concealed in wrappings
of leaf and blossom, and the tender call
of scent's inaudible crescendo trapping
my restless head into perception, sounds
resistless recollection which abounds

that instant, plural in the single brain :
as though I could become all love I lack :
pulsing and pulsing from the rose-refrain,
all unexampled kindness should come back
from where it never went, and this white rain
of petals falling down into the track
of one detained rill at the quiet side
of the warm pavement might by that decide

the one who walks to constantly renew
in all his thoughts and actions constant good :
in each correct bereftness to see through
description's coloration by its *should* :
at each step as they drop to wake anew
into perpetual daylight. Life's own food
is just food and just its just distribution
in equal love whose coming revolution

may not be image-banned, cannot not shine
in each light-emptied tain, cannot not sound
under the fixed gag of the breaking line
in which its future brilliance is bound
as colour sparkles from the white design
or as those petals cluster and drop round
in summer, as, in winter, now, the snow
descends implacably and falls below

in thickest plenty on the waiting street.
But all this happened many years ago.
In those lost days I might at each hour meet
some friend, acquaintance, past or future foe
in the next café or the fast retreat
of one room in a boarding-house : just so
the semi-circle's the verse circle where
all sit and read by turns, until, just there,

their physiognomy may either work its shape
into some single contour, some known line,
or else lose definition, fail or ape,
approximately, what is merely mine,
my dullest idiolect, the copy which can gape
its vacant resonances through each sign,
leave the two others round the table sleeping,
while the good author to himself is weeping

at each fine comma, and the candle burns
down to the pool of wax which gently hardens,
while speeches, theories, make their working turns
in earnest through each line, and sleep just pardons
his auditors : instead, perhaps, each learns
infinitesimal adjustments, gardens
of stress-flowers blooming at those unexpected
places where they should just have been rejected

and all spines shiver at the same wrong twist :
just then this novum may just not too late
retrieve new thinking from the chance it missed
& each place slides off from its former state
by minute fractions, as the beats it kissed
continuously disincinerate
the long dead poets with new wounds and gashes
restored in colours of vivacious ashes.

This ear for real sounds is like that mind
which can tell even from the latest ribbons
or from those slips in wording which it finds
in newspapers, or in those lists of givens
filed in the thick report, the very lines
of who will be killed next, who will be driven
to kill themselves, and who must leave the country
with eight slim volumes of the best and sundry

knick-knacks and small effects : a watch, a comb,
a fountain pen, a lump of bread, a dish,
a cup, one pair of shoes, a *Guide to Rome*,
some short instructions for preserving fish,
a railway timetable for Foreign, Home,
and sub-provincial services, a wish
to make one line of verse retain at last
his perfectly inoperable past.

All real experience is also stolen
from all the others with whom it was made :
as the wrong textile may not be unwoven
except its bitter colours fail and fade :
so at that edge of theft I place this colon
dividing me from what your friendly shade
thinks with me from its universal grave.
The more I steal from you, the more you have.

November at the Lamb Hotel : I am
surrounded by the fluffy little things :
on each wall, door, each doily, one sweet lamb
bleats at me mutely as its image clings
to all these surfaces, while I just cram
more notes of blankness in to where it sings
inside me with that stubborn counter-song
which I keep by me in all stupid wrong

as the indelible retrieved mnemonic
which may receive each false lamb's fancied image
from off the placard into its strong sonic
stems & fresh elements, so that this spillage
is held into resilience, this tonic
sounded beneath the big Potemkin village
of international politics or mystery
in masquerade as unresisted History :

so just these ill-drawn quadrupeds may skip,
in formula, from out their hectic frames,
in these quick lines elude the common tip
of signs & symbols, whose null switch defames
their true sublimity which at my lip
receives its catalogue of buried names
and all defeats of 1923
live as defeats once more in you and me.

Money was running out again. Why love
some certain minutes of departed charm?
You prize ferocious immanence above
all grand or tender recollection, arm
yourself against regret, will yield all of
those gone reflections, yet one little qualm
gives me pause here, since you in fact have not
those things to give me : so, then, thanks a lot.

Where did the money come from? Silence. Grey,
as though the opposite of money, stands
over and in that city where our way
leads of necessity : through these stone lands,
these streets of cashless work, our broken day
sets lines and furrows in our mortal hands
as when unweeping at the exit gate
we stare out westward to where we too late

know the new message of the falling rain
taking our faces for the empty set
which must be filled with weather yet again :
mute wail of objects, each forlorn thing set
just anywhere in space, or each swift train
rattle & scrape along a rapid set
or squeak its arc along that shining track
whose grey lifts into silver where the black

falls in the evening, and the cloud lets open
chinks in its blank mass where the hid sun lights,
white, silver, merely, as though these were spoken
from its sheer mass a human word, or spite's
compacted capital gave up one token
of whispered recognition, gave tongues rights
to live here silently behind their teeth
prisoned in tender warmth or sweet belief.

We stare towards our perfect destitution.
Europe abolishes its mind in grey
as line by line no answering restitution
comes for deletions, nor can life's shape say
what its least thought was, as the institution
of worked oblivions knows its letter day.
Its trims and tickets neatly may reset
all known thoughts back to this command : forget.

As corpse needs corpse, the one tune of your money
rings up this anthem : 'All that lives, loves life!'
I don't love all of it, nor find it funny
when I feel all of it in your blunt knife.
It's not just that it isn't milk and honey.
Life lives less than the dead whose vital strife
strikes out your wrong thought which there's no forgiving :
the dead are always less use than the living.

Thirteen, who are the cipher of re-entry,
that number which lies underneath the world,
permit me to return, you primeless sentry,
to each secreted line from which unfurled
impalpable continuations : entry
to those hid instants where all lives lie curled,
cool from your tens and threes, your sixes, sevens
that key which fits two thousand separate heavens.

Here is Zinaida in a photograph.
From what might be the surface of the moon
a jet wall rises, where one paragraph
in pale silk lets her long skirt sweep round soon :
pillar of fire in evening dress, white staff
standing to darkness from her ownmost gloom,
as though she looked towards a sunless planet
composed of silicas and helpless granite

or as that final circle which she named
in 1945 were here already,
here at the limit of her unashamed
gaze at non-love, her matchless kind & steady
attentions to despairing and defamed
souls ripped away before their all unready
thought might still ripen into some one gem
which never will be cut, if not by them.

I know that wind which blackened at her shutters
each time I lighten up & get along.
I hear it singing when I hum or mutter
for no good reason with a twice sold song.
I stand and feel it beat her, burn and cut her
just when abandoning to total wrong
each last least possible which might yet prove
the opposite of hate : non-love, non-love, non-love!

If of this woman only were remembered
her safe return into her Paris flat,
these anecdotes would be the still dismembered
limbs of the poet, as if, found like that,
each story were an incandescent ember
containing conflagrations : so that chat
might still fall silent then at one serene
look from this photograph, the breathed machine.

As when the criminal shrinks from detection
the outside of his face becomes a blur,
the flesh-felt figures of approximation
sent to derail inquiry, like what were
the opposite of conscious obligation,
the pulpy skin still longing to defer
this hour of reckoning another minute
with each weak cheek-twitch sketched or harboured in it :

so her skirt's vortex outlines the reverse,
this and just this line of revealed relation :
each swirling pleat of it effects a curse
on what would cower from its own phonation
just as each sharp line in her face speaks terse
ukases contra that disincarnation
which would send down the body to the soul,
then soul to body, and refer the whole

to some large schedule of unmeaning causes.
Is there one human face which never flinches
at any day or month, which seeks no pauses
in which to blank the real, nor finds those inches
or velvet recollections of applauses
where selfish pleasure eats its cake, then clinches
having it too, the soon too vacant stare?
Is there one face whose uncorrupted care

faced down forgetting, set its seeing look
new every second as each act unfolds
yet not to put them down inside a book
but to know how to speak a word which holds
and salves at once this wound : as though it took
whatever time it wanted, wraps or folds
pains in its painful knowing, which still sends
even attentions to those foes, now friends?

If ever I have looked upon this face
or heard its voice, it is the human word
carried in song to each part of that place
which at one distant moment was reserved
for these & just these actions, where stone's space
knows entrances & exits whose incurred
weight of true feeling sets me truly open
to hear each single word which might be spoken.

It is as though those interlocking screens
which self-defend me from one real air
slid away instantly, and what each means
were only what instead is really there
when fifteen ornaments recede : each weans
me from its counter-milk, the frozen glare
of information. I cannot choose choice.
The song falls silent, and I hear your voice.

You are the catalogue of proper names,
the mouth which shapes them, and the line which bends
each stream of breath to bear shame's shaded shames;
you are the prayer-wheel, and what it mends
with revolutions; yours those equal flames
consuming capitals, & yours what tends
those fires in life : you love, make, send and are
this whole word, this unintermitting star.

The list of those promotions which let stress
rest at an instant where it else might choke
thought's necessary breath : you are no less
than fresh gales rain-filled to disperse that smoke
which blocks the throat's own thinking : you address
your unstopped vocative, note's over-croak
to that woke ear which lets its hearing be
tuned to the uninterrogable sea.

You are the ocean : you are what exceeds
all strictest limits, yet at last contains
that rich restriction-list which still impedes
blank generality, or sets refrains
to sing where limits' limit supersedes
to singularity, since its bright gains
are always also no less shining losses,
scoured plinths and blocks which yet require their mosses.

So lyric beating its essential bounds
in uncontainable desire of more
as one archaic quantity astounds
to quality of rhyming, then puts your
frame of attentions in its proper grounds,
its home-felt territories, flung contour
of ineliminable unblocked questions
whose intonations are the sung suggestions

making the substance of the unknown world :
you are each tree and flower, since this little
lift of your voice at phrase end would unfurl
the undeleted logic of sheer spittle
in whose wet resonances skulks that curled
paradise-pedantry whose jot and tittle
is the foundation of the firmament
returning mere inks to the thought they meant.

A prose descent is kept behind the set.
Yet, when I come down, I retain this felt
series of interlinkings; when I get
a glass of water or just watch ice melt
there at my room's edge, I am not unmet
by each incorporated mediation
whose buried history is still what spelt
seeming immediacy's superannuation.

Chu, kolokol poet pro dal'nij breg
or hear the car alarm which squeals in panic :
as though the thing had lost an arm or leg
ripped from its circuitry, it cheeps these manic
inefficacious peals, or cash would beg
the very poor it grinds to fix satanic
locks and protections to the shrink wrapped food
just from the hungry, or shut up the good

inside these wonderful machines, to shine
like wax fruit, poisoned. No one turns a hair.
I see them walking past its world's-end whine
knowing this untongue shreds the tender air
in perfect meaninglessness. Each bent tine
sits on the gone key. Folk ignore it where
it howls and yammers, yet cannot be heard,
because it may not say a single word.

The counter-bell, the opposite of sounding :
the contrary of a discrete occasion :
the noise of nothing, sin's squeaked anti-founding :
the false free tempering without contagion :
the whistle whistling down all first lived grounding :
the tiny slow continuous abrasion
of all resources from exhausted trust,
expending all durations into dust :

a noise it is impossible to hear :
an auditory symbol, whose swift click
tranfers you instantaneously here
at that null now-point when its single trick
makes time go space-shaped, drowns in total fear
all real perception, and prefers to stick
a phonic label on the wax-packed ear
until whatever might be heard as dear

speaks the no language of these mocked up tones.
You can alone out-think it : you whose ears
were stuffed with gooseberries when heavy stones
were laid upon the bells, and whose snapped years
creep back to 1918, when the phones
at last consumed all ringing, which appears
since then to bring its merely private clangour
to scratch some itch, or gratify some languour.

Your grandfather had known the bells of Chud.
A tune made out of very diminution
of re-sonations, as from bronze to wood,
so that the zenith of its elocution
was just the thinnest, driest note, which should
exult subtractively in resolution
its poor clunk on the board which could release
richest ideas at its sound's decease.

The microrhythms of these hectic pulses
are as a cavalry to Rome's thick tread :
its reckless dashes, unprechecked impulses,
bring all to prayer from the softest bed :
from stationary metal these repulses
of dexterous hammers ring the clever dead
up to their stations of immortal silver
where rung elations from that fixed rank fill the

air with processions of competing chimings
whose emulous antagonisms join
in sweetest interruptions, where strange timings
make nature's art a nature, or the line
of thronged ascetics, whose most strenuous idlings
collect battalions into this fine
host of corrected self-self-appositions
struck from luck's temper to these ringing fissions.

The poet is the one-man North Korea.
His thorax shakes continuously with stress
held against stress, idea against idea;
his head blocks entry to what would confess
the failure of his line : he ranks by fear
that inner regiment whose shouts may press
each thought or phoneme to its loyal service
in perfect freedom from whoever heard this.

Get disconnected, since the only vent
for airs & graces is the severed cable :
only at that point where the web is rent
is this collective apparatus able
to see one colour, clock one distant scent
or sit at a completely empty table :
switch off the pictures, clear the virid links
each gene would grab for from the thing which thinks.

A bell suspended in the summer air
effects this interruption to discursive
concatenations of false persons where
each figurine blinks up the blank recursive
totem of self, emoticon's despair
shuttling away from thought with every cursive
screen-tendered send-off of extent's dead scribble,
this electronic counterpart of dribble :

a bell, the unsurrendered idiophone,
corrects and tears this fabric, puts a block
on vacant commerce, when each liquid tone
gushes & tumbles from the neck : true clock
whose watch can't see the wrist, day's bone
which holds the spirit up, month's sounding stock,
you call and call across the faithless state
unheard and unremembered till too late.

Seven to bless the waters, five to call
me to my work, and ten to mark the passion,
twice for the priest, four for the funeral,
six at the day's end, thrice to fill or fashion
the first commencement, the event, or fall
to seventy or eighty whose impassioned
repeated peals are the declared alarm
both signaling and dispelling harm.

It is walled up with lilies and rosettes,
never to speak of sacring any more;
its former turrets and its parapets
lack those inhabitants which were before
permitted to inform you when bread gets
remade-irradiated at that door
which opens every day from inexplicable
stuff which lights stuff up as the inextricable

diamond of questions, as the hardest known
substance we find here : so each blackbird's soul
breaking melismas out inside the stone
carols and descants down that unreal whole
abolished now by that which is alone
real as this matter of a living coal
burning implacably the stolen nations
in the long blaze of its interrogations.

The two big bells worked by the foot at Caen :
the tower shook enough to make you sea-sick.
Cast all your silver in the furnace : shone
glints of that element will light its music.
The long nomenclature of all long-gone
baptized & shriven ringers clangs aphasic
bleeps, plinks and whistles to their proper times,
tolling them back home to their native chimes,

so that, in this dark room, I hear the light
roars of continuous combustion float
up to my perch, & now I hear them right.
They are not altogether strange; their note
drifts like an index, not an icon, flight
of what lay buried in deep strata, throat
of trees compressed into those rich & black
fuels & powers, to let each burning track

go past in just this journey far below.
It's still the same earth, still this frozen rock.
Our thought disincarnation may not go
so far as to dispel, refuse or block
our foot's print, or to dissipate in show
those little noises which still come to knock
here at the oval window of the ear
where I am stranded in some thick unclear

woods & dense matters, where the only clearing
requires that axe which always had already
been set to make it, so that this appearing
tarmac of total culture is the steady
oblivion of labour, whose quick hearing
listens at each edge of the still unsteady
city for those reviving beats & demons
coming round slowly to these counter-Edens.

Culture is murder. When you build a house,
it is a zone of killing for what lived
there previously; emmet, worm and mouse
are razed thus sacredly, then must forgive
these violent triumphs of all zealous nous
from where, in wooden effigy, they give,
ventriloquized, their blessing to that species
which files their corpses with its junk and faeces.

Yet murder is not culture, since the house
cannot be built by killing. Must this sieve
mesh out nine tithes of life, must cat and mouse,
if they would think, learn love and hatred, give,
in these continuous holocausts to nous,
one burnt part over, one part to forgive?
Can there be culture without sacrifice?
I doubt it, but, at all events, the ice

will vanish long before we can find out,
and if there is no culture is your brag,
you'll have it, richly, when the drowning spout
of new Deucalion inundates each crag
or last kept pinnacle of thinking : doubt
as mesh & torrent make each least thought sag
and find it idiotic or just funny
to draw one breath which does not rhyme with money,

which reminds me that I haven't fed the meter
and has me just for once up on my feet
to get the right coins for it, so the heater
won't shut down suddenly, and sour these sweet
reflections upon snow, &c.,
into that cold which always will defeat a-
n idyll of any kind, make sweet verse bleat
Just turn the boiler on, &c.

The Melodies of Russian Lyric Verse
was written in a flat which lacked all heating.
Graphs of hit pitches silently rehearse
mouth's laws and lawfulness, the tunes of eating;
dream of art's sciences, the shiny curse
spoken and spoken over each too fleeting
rhythm of thinking, till the poor bird's head
is known exhaustively, and left for dead.

I am not feeling altogether well.
You have accompanied me to this far
interior of scissions : you repel
wrong influences by those lines which are
cut out inside you, as I still retell
this count twice through to the unlistening star
shining and shining where I cannot see
its light reflected in an absent sea.

These spiritual exercises fill
intolerable vacancy, whose dark
matter is waiting just beyond my sill,
or frolics lawlessly across the park :
with each eight's matrix I may more than kill
intolerable sleeplessness; each mark
keeps me awake so that, beneath its cedar,
I may bring sleep to you, my loyal reader.

No other eye has made it to this line.
We are alone here. Don't you, therefore, fear
that, in this solitude, I may confide
some secret to you, whose reviled idea
you may find you cannot forget? The mind
has oceans, yet they cannot wash, from clear
hatred & terror, all worst hours of pain
more than it may resolve for joy, or chain

proposed prose outlines to persisting verse.
Why would I do this? What I want instead
is that these little clicks might still reverse
continuous compulsory forgetting
of the true, good & beautiful, uncurse
those interdicted transcendentals, said
ubiquitously to be too upsetting,
until they once more settle in the head :

world without end of these still inextirpable
illuminations of their inadmissible
anticipations of that unattainable
disincantation of unparaphrasable
exacerbation of all indecipherable
ciphers of paradise whose ineliminable
wish holds its true attention to the dark
background of light, its unabraded mark.

I must re-open the supplanted places.
This means remeasuring the books, since they
contain, unproperized, those very faces,
sunk in the staff of ink, which want to say
not only what you tabulate, but graces
recompositionally pitched so they
refuse to move, retreat, revise or flinch
till the whole world look different by one inch.

The codes themselves contain their living thoughts.
Revive them with dissection, since each limb
wakes up when cut : from their forlornest forts
each several word returns the printed hymn
to voice-propulsions. To their proper ports
each tone-refloated vessel may come in
exacting every concept's strong exertions
against sin's strong sleep and its blank desertions.

The stock of propers has run short again.
They may not be made up, but must arrive
from close attention to some shape of pain
captured in paper-traps & served alive
in differentiations of refrain
whose repetitions gather, switch and drive
to those true publicly enstated writings
which unwrong law's song with belated rightings.

Who could invent the office of the dead?
It could not not be made up, now each word
bears its proprietor inside it, bled
dry to that chatteldom in which each heard
gesture or tongue-twist owns one sovereign head.
Each knows its master, each word is referred
back to its patent, to those first possessors
who stole it from the common of confessors.

So each must die; so each cold bit of language
is alien capital, and just to trade it
is zeal to found that total counter-language
which rips each word off from that church which made it
or severed tongue to fill the bloody sandwich
who put it on a plate and then displayed it
with the gone monument of vile suppressions,
rich disavowals and dim intercessions.

It is the same for libraries and shops.
It is as though salvation might be tied
to transient accident, to counter-tops
& matt black baffle boards, & then denied
just as the next initiative just lops
all these known features from the shop's inside :
as though a human life were an ecstatic
self-self-expulsion to this automatic

pattern of ratified eradications
dissolving each thing I might come to know :
as though what must be crossed out from the nations
were each familiar place where I might go :
to be replaced with identifications :
where I side instantly with what I know
will slash, burn, blank, and send me to the dark
so that in this way I may make my mark.

In a pocket at the bottom of its window
boards so provide that every point of light
may be absorbed, may vanish : so the window
sweeps in a concave curve from left to right
where vitrolite and chrome surrounds the window
whose non-reflective glass brings me in tight
in bound absorption to the bright umbrellas
which step their stationary tarantellas

there in the window, where all light comes home
to homeless money's lit-unliving offer.
This power destroys the previously known :
the daylight-lamps' twelve thousand candles proffer
a rage of phosphorescence, blazing zone
wheedling & yammering from that bright coffer.
They shrink the front to let me on these floors
walk through to frameless armour-plated doors :

I must accept the offer, or shrink back
into ungenerous and failed resistances :
this meal of light expels to final lack
whoever disbelieves its white existences :
the lights inside the plastic box signs track
these leavers' shadows, till their thin consistencies
are shone through thoroughly, & known to hold
no substance that might be compared with gold.

These verticals were my Helvellyn : these
apparent permanences could not but
become my pattern of delight and ease
from which it follows that when each one shut
I saw the mountain tremble, knew disease
run through each absolute, and learnt to cut
all ties of spirit. Never stay the same :
I must be liquidated to this name.

So winglike volutes sprout from copper-clad
columns keeled forward to support the lintel :
a wall of glass refuses to be sad,
shows the dark store behind it, while with mental
pain I walk slowly to where I am had
in equal palaces of ornamental
socks, sofas, lampstands, coffee tables, stuff
reminding me that I can never have enough.

Long poems are anthologies of lines.
Anthologies are made by devastations.
As gold is brought up from the fatal mines
by sticks & stones, and not by sweet orations,
so words culled out by tunes still curve the spines
of all who bring them up, expectorations
of throat's one formula which burns and burns
to fuel each thought and story from its turns.

They will not sit still in the shining window.
It is to you they call and call in vain.
From backlit paper whose recessed thin glow
pushes them up, again and still again
they call you to them, they desire to go
walking through each blocked footpath of your brain
until they are its substance as those actual
tissues & sparks which even you call factual.

The poem is the single arc of tone,
not a selection : so, where you relent,
permitting fragments of the merely known
to be inserted, then the line is sent
down broken-backed into the fissured bone
whose fracture must be healed with that right rent
which severs a prosthesis from your nerve,
retrieves the true flight of your healing curve.

Each must outlive his line : each voice must know
its own spoke choking, know sick iridescence,
eye filled with oil, because the tongue can't go
one inch without it taste self-obsolescence.
Each meets a part of dust which is to show
the just-perduring speaker his senescence :
since the recalled notes of 1911
will not pay this day's passage to its heaven.

What could once sorcerously shape-change, line
still insusceptible to points, breaks down;
what once distributed to ours each mine
stiffens, a grimace in the wind, or frown
fixed, idiotically, where my spine
peters out headwards : the deserted town.
More silenced even than Blondel or Loisy
is Konstantin Bal'mont who died at Noisy.

His followers were scattered and dispersed.
Every least reader can forget him : each knows how
just to require a better line of verse
since each knows not to babble, each may, now,
fetch specificity, log, do no worse
than keen transcription of detritus, bow
to each stern captain of idoloclasm.
Each may leap clear of each once fearful chasm,

as he was driven to the western sea,
as a leaf fallen on its furthest shore
or wave-obliterated shell may be
again revealed by its withdrawing roar
like the left monument from which there flee
unknowing tides, until the sea once more
cover all record of that sounding curl
or beat into the sand what might unfurl

in shells' flesh images, the metropolitan
cult antitype of this recluded hut :
marine where limestones find their final polishing
at the dead centre, although each be cut
at the harsh margin, whose once cosmopolitan
selected rubbish cast up on the shut
rock exit ragged at this edge of oceans
bears in its crags each toothmark of their motion,

brought back to Paris in a taxi cab
to meet the doctor, be pronounced insane,
degenerate, rave, drink, desire to stab
each bright competitor, fall down again,
wax sentimental, drink again, then blab
secrets it kept for sixty years : feel pain,
without remarking it, in every muscle,
know sheer defeat in every junked corpuscle.

Now it is raining. Since I cannot see,
from this fixed chair, the outside world, I trust
these sounds of rain which make their way to me
as though a handful of some sand or dust
were thrown against the pane. Now I am free
from that illusory event : I must
know now that nothing can be known as sent,
but each just falls somewhere like the unmeant

totality of accident. It falls.
It may no longer be received as speech.
It just descends, and on the roof and walls
its tapped arrivals neither sing nor teach,
pure noise emancipated from those calls
which make sounds, symbols. So, now, each by each,
the drops drip softly on the spattered top,
as though I might permit myself to stop,

yet falter, hesitating, at that minute
when I might cease or cease forever, let
another little thought come, linger in it,
till, like a puddle, it expand, and get
me counting, and I may not unbegin it,
but travel from this raindrop to the met
edge of a question, and its struckthrough first,
friendly companion of the very worst :

so that I cannot think the rain could whisper,
knock, strike, beat, hammer, since a human verb
corrodes rain's rain-intentions; aspidistra
never rain-kissed, or delicate cloched herb,
demand rain-verbs to catch its single glister,
that scent awoken in the rain-lack kerb
when after thirty weeks of rainless weather,
it knows ten drops of rain which fall together,

not, as I, now, three hundred thousand dropping
into the wet conjectured street below
where they rain down into the still unstopping
river of vehicles which has to go
downstream towards those centres where the shopping
has to be done, as all flesh has to know
it is as grass or as some surplus plastic
whose wish to be there simply is fantastic.

I set a watchman to my mouth : I tell
each hour in silence, while the rain-clock drizzles
these wetter seconds, & the drowning bell
muffles its clangours, or a rocket fizzles,
fails to ignite, collapses. I too well
know these short episodes, when damped fire sizzles
and I am left thus incommunicado,
a Dresden figure of El Desdichado.

Nocturnal panoplies of mute allusion!
In here, I may not see that nod or wink
whose prolix eyelid should to blank confusion
flip my blind soul, de minimis : its blink,
propels me to, deflects me from, delusion,
since, irreversibly, this shutter thinks
thoughts of the properly demure left thumb
uttered in Cluniac, the hand-strapped tongue.

The finger's syntax is a breaking wave
which never can be stilled : each item points
contrastive dances which may dash or save
those limbs which trip them, since inflected joints
step thus collected to the sense they crave
whose nail is paralanguage, which appoints
contingencies of bitterness as trapping
our stared attentions in its protein wrapping,

so I imagine, in this gapless dark.
Is there a woman's hand so beautiful
that babes shut up inside the womb might mark
and leap for bliss at it, or one sweet cuticle
whose extra-gestural remainder, lark
of musculature, should in dutiful
colours of semaphore make melt with joy
each born immortal, each womb-hidden boy?

Are there hand-canticles? May digits sing
in agile numbers how the proud are scattered,
or inclinations of the forehead bring
their signalled musics to the slow or rapid
silent processionals? Is there a thing
which thinks, a mind which ever matters,
or is the world emphatically nothing,
this wrecked perfection which can rhyme with nothing?

Babes at the breast give kisses of the lips
to glad the queen of heaven when she gave
suck to the blissful child; but when her ships
come sailing into paradise, that wave
will bear still sweeter kisses, since his lips
will kiss her mouth in welcome, as all crave
this shining top of happy solidarity,
this flesh-met zenith of denuded charity.

Stand off, you mountains that once flowed with milk.
You hills, depart, that poured forth streams of honey.
I am empowered to commission silk
just on condition that I burn the money
and drown its ashes. Where that drink is spilt
forever shadows, there, upon the sunny
hillside, remain : the mouth of the dead lion
gives up refreshments through the whole of Zion.

The lip's door opens, but no human sounds
may come out from it, since the cold angelic
signals displace them. Each pure tone rebounds
in pre-recorded resonance; each relic
bears its lit signature, whose trick redounds
on the long crypt of would-be autotelic
trills, blinks, clicks, whistles, or salvation's noises
offered for sale as though they were just choices.

His voice could break the cedar, but this sets
a thousand chainsaws on the saw-sown forest.
He put the heresies to flight : this bets
on one word's margin, variants in Horace.
His goings shall not slide, but sliding gets
more going for us, whispers, now, be honest,
of the long harmonies he then expounded,
which of them can at all today be sounded?

Today, tonight, I may sound what I like
here in this quite inefficacious room.
Privation's offer is an open mic.
I turn it down, since this persistent gloom
blocks out the blocks, and what you just dislike
may still be uttered. Never ask to whom
a human word is spoken & delivered :
you are yourself that neck where first it shivered.

You are the alpha and omega; you
are one, and are each number which exceeds it :
you are that pointing, punctuation who
breathes for me, and the page which still succeeds it :
you are the pen which strikes my writing through,
the grace-felled poem, and the face to read it.
Do not ask, after this, then, what to do.
Who am I writing for? For whom but you.

From toast to telegram : you raise your glass
to disappearance, since you must go down
into refining fire. You coldly pass
through these fierce temperatures, set your frown,
all which is presaged in this act, this last
small vessel lifted to the others. Sound
dwindles, from glossolalias, to sparser
spells & their texts on this Hentinerstraße.

It is as though this little wrist's ascent
or lights refracting in the lifted cup
were by your hushed speech chilled and hallowed, lent
force of forced action when the hand goes up
convoking twenty spirits, with its meant
injunction, to produce, in that they sup,
true recognition of this offered fiction,
your dream of literary crucifixion.

Just as your iris might from glass collect
pictures in little of all those who sit
at the rejected table, and select
these images to be displayed in it,
since friends and enemies alike reflect
here in your staring pupil, each now lit
or dark miscellany of Russia's others,
as though this gaggle were a band of brothers :

so might your fingers lifting by an inch
bright fluids to the disbelievers make
their shared experience that you don't flinch
the thing which makes it difficult to take
your word for lost breath when the state should lynch
illegal poets, have and eat its cake,
as, at some junctures, it is best, or, safer,
to keep a pocket for the proffered wafer.

If you believe that spirits can't disperse
in this way through their objects, then just think
how when at wits' end you may barely nurse
your thoughts from one day to the next's thick blink
or even find the way from bad to worse
then, from a room of books, their buried ink
reviving in you every mind forsaken
may with its silent bindings reawaken

entire collectives in my sleepy head.
Switch all the pronouns : from this one room ring
yours, mine, theirs, ours, because this single bed
lies in the sight of all those spines which sing
their individual histories, unsaid
mnemonics of incarcerated spring.
Each kind of cloth retains its special power
to reproduce in full some certain hour;

or would do, if it were not perfect night.
Now, as I look, although I cannot see,
I know where each stands on the shelf in light.
I recollect them where they may not be
seen or interpreted : I hear each right,
hearing their proper voices, until we
speak up by listening into the dark,
write in auditions of this printed ark.

Repel from the caliginous interior
its dusks & dimnesses : as this black night
has drained all colours from its dark exterior,
bring me once more into the single right
path of illumination, my superior.
Hold me now movelessly into the light.
I look towards it. It is 2 a.m.
I may not see it now; until you bend

me to its new rays, I just sit here crawling
in spirit, while my frame remains as still
as any stone oblivious to the calling
of what if it might only listen will
coax it to life, because what is not falling
pushes a word up and across the sill
into the ever distant street outside
which I may see whenever I have died.

I from a single line of foreign verse
sleeping between safe covers on the shelf
may by this trick of memory reverse
part of the damage to my mastered self :
since it is always good to know the worst
I must release some undeceiving elf
to wake one lapsed connection in my head
with the assistance of the written dead.

Then even from this capital of cold
I may resume auroras of September.
I call the predecessors of that gold
whose leaf dies finely first in dim November
to bring autumnal tremors from these old
pavements and windows, since this white December
may by one little syllable revert
to its first inkling, as a face were hurt

as imperceptibly by that more cool
air drifting past it, or were brought to know
in that brief moment like a waking fool
summer's swift exit, and what has to go
shivered on skin then when the dusk-brushed pool
hardens to ridges with the wind-pushed flow
and its dark waters pull the day's late light
downward inevitably into night :

when at the same time sweetest comfort wakens
into the burnt head, and I walk along
as though domestic items, cups and kettles,
were each repositories of some strong
unbreakable contentment, or those metals
brought all the work in them to proper song
and these calm passions might outshine excess,
completely unexpected happiness.

Then it is gone. One night succeeds another.
One shone invisibly, before the next
repeals the findings of its elder brother.
I read them out until the hidden text
shuttles, defunct, from one side to the other.
It never speaks to me, is never vexed,
but is reprinted from sheer inanition
identically without a new edition.

Even the saltatricious decollations
proceed in perfectly unruffled calm.
Even its meretricious exclamations
upon bad nudity of some girl's arm
are born in silence, like examinations.
This apparatus for preventing harm
knows its spring, summer, autumn, winter parts
and catalogues their still subservient arts.

Ambrose commands I should drink from the neck
what cannot satisfy my starving heart.
Still through the far seas swims the foundered wreck.
This oceanic page without a chart
lies blank before me : I am sail and deck,
hull, mast and standard, since my numbered art
is driven by no breath of air but you,
who are my pilot and my lost crew too.

Deleted feasts I celebrate by fasting,
fasts I still feast through in this equal train
of soldered disconnections, whose unlasting
phantasmagorias process again
in eulogies to zero : each nil gasping
till its successor in the soul-reft brain
arise to die, and send to void durations
infinitesimal annihilations.

Decapitation is the state religion,
since the republic of free dancing girls
transits from banquets to the bitter prison
where at each place it rapidly unfurls
the other's flag, for what is once arisen
must be brought down, as though all graceful curls
required that God's blood never must be shed,
the better to once more cut off his head.

I live the sequence of defenestrations.
Each little impulse wants to throw away
whatever makes repulsive demonstrations
of its determinacy, or would say
its name in public, let its obligations
block up the circuit and get in the way
of natural malice, as though each would dash
to pieces everything which is not cash.

Oak peacocks, thrust your uncorrupted beaks
immortally into their wooden chalice!
Set from surrendered Cappadocian peaks
these carved parts of an unremitting palace!
So thought's caught avians, its tree-fixed freaks
repel still, by these crests, unconscious malice,
& on the neighbouring A590
queues grind to halts before they find their hero.

Since Nineveh and since Persepolis
find their continuators in these measures
of everlasting placards, whose metropolis
discursifies all meadows, puts its treasures
for numbers of the never-sent cosmopolis,
then works up furiously its count of pleasures
into asphaltic infrastructures, or
just fails to tell you what the thing is for,

so are these ancient empires overcome
better in limestone, where the sacred phoenix
gains a Greek date-palm, and these chunks of dumb
incarcerated sacrifice let Kleenex
float by in bits like white remains of some
province of royal waste, a law whose remits
make, of each level sand, a standing dump,
or sap each leapt dance to a casual slump.

I cannot bear to look into its eye.
I do not need to, since I cannot see it.
Here, in this deepest darkness, I still spy
that fifty-folded quire. I may not be it,
yet strain each muscle to this end : that my
invulnerable tongue be wounded, free it,
& each ledge loose its griffin-throat to sing
its each own name, its undiminished thing.

It is an eloquence inaudible
at any single listening : it throngs
with bounding line, yet is invisible
to any single glance, and yet its songs
are at the same time indivisible
in supersession of collected wrongs
buried & saved & conquered in this ark
whose least best beast still thinks into the dark.

These are the three boys singing in the furnace.
Here at this poem's midnight, I hear bright
notes of asbestos, where the spirit learns its
parts of invincible attack, since white
heat would cremate them, yet may only turn its
resurgent rages on itself. This night
shelters that molten voice in coolest dew,
as all my properties just melt in you.

Continuous instruction to adore
the golden skyscraper may be refused
simply by failing to adore it, or
remembering this simply disabused
instant of knowledge, when the unheard roar
of many engines meets the ear as news
of this and just this real noise of damage
beyond all power to disinvent or manage :

so the three trebles from their hot detention
pipe up antiphoners of matched set blessing,
as highest notes from deepest held retention
of each historiated letter, guessing
its own dark future of restrained intention
and with its arsenals of hue confessing
those benedictions of the frost & ice
sung by leviathans and dolphins twice.

The sun knows when to set. Your real action
shrinks to a book, from whence it may not yet
get up and walk, because its lone redaction
proscribes those dances which might still be met
in favour of this lonely satisfaction :
this private primer, this unlikely bet
whose real faith is in annihilation.
I read it patiently towards cremation.

The lucernarium is shadowed; light
cowers in sodium, as if that glass
were fifty thousand chancel screens, whose right
were put away from flesh, which, as the grass,
must only burn up, if this deepest night
were to bear torches. So we merely pass.
The whole world's store of fuel is privated,
just so we may not doubt we are belated.

Fear of the dark inhabits undiminished
these trains of sponsored lights, these intercessors,
these points and spirals of a still unfinished
web of repression, these lit nonconfessors,
these counter-comminations which would finish
all times & seasons, like the poor possessors
of one invariance of grey duration,
one self-sold minute, one ejected nation.

Cut up the pie, then eat it all yourself :
this was the smashers' maxim. So the font
goes unblest, or defaced. They drink a health
to abolitions of all need & want,
then pocket picas, with some other wealth,
eventually to end up in Vermont,
in a vitrine, with one poor page held open,
of these privations the too precious token.

Photismal baptisms! I crawl towards
your tanks and pools of light : I may step in,
since these immersions are the still rewards
of long agrypniai; wash off my sin;
reverse that ratchet in me which awards
false permanences to the worst; begin
light's office to me in this utter black,
real plenitudes to my pretended lack.

A dog barks in the street. One living sound
may reach me, even here; air's one remark,
spoken off-handedly, may be the ground
of real renewals; so the blackened park,
which I know to exist, yet have not found
my way to, lets this listenable spark
through to my chair, to this fixed seat of error,
this still repeating prophylact for terror.

The little hand which moves around the clock
sends through my silent room its violent crashes,
as though its accurate and patient tock
lacked a light tick, or as though clock-clacked lashes
nailed me down here, as both securely locked
to no known mast, and also with these ashes
waxed to the gunwales, blinded, bound & gagged,
maxed to all purposelessness, tied & bagged.

I ring with pulses, since the more I miss
each extra messenger, the more I may
know, of each instant, just its special kiss,
its curse, its contour, its peculiar way
of passing and of failing, its soft hiss,
its tremors, exhalations : and the day
awaits me anyway, the light will come,
so I am promised by this deaf and dumb

hour of the page, this alcohol-based ink,
this flexing letter which reminds me how
I often may remember that I think.
You are exactly half way through it now.
Perhaps you have deserved a little drink?
Here at the centre of this earth I vow
my heart and kidneys to you, since you read
& resurrect me in each print-sepultured creed.

I mean to die in 1895.
I choose September, when the century
a little cools. The wish to be alive
is mingled with another wish : to be
absorbed into the misty park, or drive
through rowan clusters, where each dusk-drowned tree
draws me still further through the twilight park
until last glimmers fade to perfect dark

and I am solitary, happy, lost
in that deep grove of silent pine and birch,
taking the wrong path through the many-mossed
roots, stumps and rocks, those muds, where fir and larch
mutely know nothing of my walk, whose cost
I now no longer count, and my spent torch
can show me nowhere, as the thick black sky
wields perfect lightlessness, and by and by

I slow, I stumble, I sit down to rest;
I let myself recline upon a bank
right in the middle of the park, and guess
how long it will be now, and, silent, thank
whatever power has brought me to this best
of disappearance, to this rich and dank
home of Septembers. I escape rebirth,
sleeping for ever in the happy earth.

This tune comes to me at that time of year
without fail, when the wind across my arm
reminds me wordlessly of this sweet fear
which need not threaten any real harm,
but that of ending : whose fleet signs appear
just in the very advent of a calm
change in the sounds of movements in the street,
an altered resonance of people's feet,

the way the door shuts with a different noise
from that it had in summer. Each perception
binds me so gently, with its little toys,
into my coming death. There's no deception.
Life holds its permanence of certain joys
just in mortality : proprioception
governs no feeling, and I fall and cease
for ninety years along this lived release.

I still recall those winter afternoons
and how they dipped and darkened into dusk;
through the west window into those wide rooms
a grey light fell, then vanished, leaving just
one low lamp in the corner, while these glooms
deepened around us like the truth which must
receive us each insuperably there
to last oblivions beyond repair :

but that before each thread of light had gone
from the tall windows, it had dropped and shimmered
on the long table, where these few shards shone
for some brief minutes with a blaze not dimmer
but raising fugitively fire from on
the burnished surface of the wood which glimmered
just at that moment when your voice still trembled
as though by listening we were assembled

into sodality whose lasting word,
although it never could be known, would speak
under the ground one real note, unheard
from that first twilight, till at last it greet
the silent strata like some undeferred
sent benediction, & its worn-out feet
might in this absence of a path find best
recumbance & unutterable rest.

That single instant of your voice convoked
collected wordlessness to silent speaking :
as though one wobble in your throat revoked
all resignation, all thought of retreating,
or with its subtle tremors there awoke
forgotten resolutions from their sleeping
tuned several deliveries to shine
as indivisible in your sung line.

So that we sat around the room at least
as though the westward cheeks of our lit faces
found in your voice their unseen blazing east
where in thought's undersong some viewless traces
still knew the melodies for each least feast,
still with their strong lines kept the ancient places
spared & recovered, as the stone cold nut
retains one needful manual in shut

incalculable burial, since its
refusing adoration sets a block
stopping mere nature where it dumbly sits
under the tarmac, & no human clock
may reach its meant intentions, till in fits
it sends lent tendrils, like a living shock :
just as pain breaks the false tongue's stony track,
so from the dead this dead word stumbles back.

The street is a museum of deletions.
Should I walk out along this public road,
I feed my freedoms from the bitter regions
packed underneath the cables : where what showed
one living gesture, makes up those repletions
refusing feast and fast. So I implode
the calendar into this strip of times
walked & used up by me : I muffle chimes

into indifferent continuation.
Thick lines of paint along the tar implore
my acquiescence in elimination
of all directions which were known before :
as though the comic substance of a nation
took flight into this evanescent store
of place-names placarded, the fixed angelic
example toponym, whose little relic

stands for a city floating in the air.
Its life is magical : it is invisible :
there is no sense in which this town is there
more than a grain of sand could be divisible
until it multiply, a thousandth share
of thousandths, & its sign efface all visible
pavements and courtyards with this air-sent net,
this wireless kingdom of the wrong not-yet.

A neutral ideality, a mind
stripped of cognitions, since its empty set
is still distributed : it knows no kind
but from this ether has the blank rush let
all fantasized indifferences find
their aerial element, their sightless debt
consume the gone interior of each thing
till all lack match back in a gapless ring.

So that the merest little object can
become peculiarly alive, since not
convertible into this code. I ran
along the street, between the ranks of hot
cars, trucks & motorcycles, and began
to see this extra in the least lost jot
of silenced architecture : fixed foot-super
turned to the kerb or feed-line where the looper

drops as a console to the stone tie-beam
or stairscape written up across the square
cuts out the handrail, makes its low steps seem
the deck of levels which above prepare
its invitation to ascent, no dream
but shared experience of what is there
as evident constraint, yet also open
to sun's bright flicker where their line is broken.

I hear your breathing through the whole held night.
I stand now, painfully, and watch your closed
eyelids pulse lightly in the dark, as might
were resting there, or you were counterposed
in thinking blindness to excess of bright
hospital fluorescence, flesh opposed
in flat recalcitrance of sleeping life
to the syringe or delicate kind knife

which could prolong your consciousness of pain.
The breath you take into your mouth requires
an exhalation, and you once again
draw to your failing lung what still inspires
your unintelligible thoughts : domain
of all dead sectors where no mind respires
yet something moves, yet something is alive
still in this failing carapace to thrive.

I hear each cup of air process and drop.
I hear you draw them from the solemn sphere
so that from this last peak, your still frame's top,
they go down gently, & reviving dear
breath seems to fill you or to never stop
while at your side I am as if not here
accompanying each attempt at living
with those constructions which I still am giving

to each least sign of life, each tick or rattle
when the expelled flow breaks the teeth's seal back :
each feint or venture in the head's met battle
when it lies still or shakes, grows or contracts :
each lash, each nostril, hair, mask, tube or chattel
pinned to your face until its saving track
ends nowhere, and at last you are cut free
to spend this darkest night alone, with me.

You rock with breathing, since its amplitude
diminishes in just that fashion which
makes quietness, an emphasis : as nude
parts of your blank face lose each singling glitch
marking out thoughts, until desuetude
advances calmly, or you throw some switch
sending your whole face to an inexpressive
mass of pale tissue or the soft recessive

retreat of sentience, your final passing.
Now is an almost perfect stillness there.
You barely move, as though you were amassing
the world's reserves of rest, and would not share
one instant of relief, or lose, in passing,
one moment's silence, as you slow to where
you will in some near future be discovered
never to be revived, known, or recovered.

For now your breathings mark my path of time
on through the night, and, as they rise and fall,
I tune my thoughts; I damp each rising chime
when you subside, and bid each over-tall
pitch drop to depths from which it will not shine
more than a dun patch. So your lungs' last call
protracts itself from second to linked second
outlasting each time more than may be reckoned.

These are the flowers of the very desert.
Breathe without ceasing, since this single strand
perpetuating an unmingled measure
spins your breath out into the whole strung band,
this choral solitude, this sole shared treasure
repeated always to the hearing sand
as though one building might contain the strength
to match the world out for the world's whole length.

Without this fortress of renunciation
the rest goes fallen, and the left profane
usurps the lot for its denunciation,
razing in zeal each shadow of a fane
from which might come unmixed annunciation
that nature's causal total know one lane,
one cut or byway not foreseen or bought,
one chink, one adit, one remain, one thought.

So in the Quonset hut I see your bulk
heaved to endurances, to one more terce,
one more and then one more, the counter-sulk,
lifelong self-emptying to this stripped first,
this single riddle, this revived gone hulk,
as though each canticle were set to nurse
life through life's loss, life's life through life's surrender,
or constant watering might make stones tender.

Lay down your pen : decline to write this word,
since its worn cloth will fray before you set
its many letters on the skin. You heard :
play from your strip of ink no more signs met
in walking through the worst; keep one unheard
series of sounds inside the skull, then let
this single atom leap to leaves and branches,
this cold necessity explode in chances.

Be still : it is just nothing, which you do,
and, when you've done it, then the rest have, too.
Fall silent : it is someone else's hymn;
the night defeats you, as the dust does him.
Shut down your box : no sandbank may contain
this helpless quantity of salt and rain.
Then from still silence and the shut down head
learn what you always had already said.

Rolled opal is impervious to blood.
I think beside you how a single pleat
might stand between you and whatever mud
might interject itself, or with its sweet
infection penetrate : whose fatal bud
were here averted by hygienic fleet
lights' unmeant flickers in the slab of glass
through which no fragment of the air may pass.

Here in the dark I crave those towers of light
whose thousand fluted sheets are fixed in iron
so that illuminated spheres fall right,
in curved grids dropping on the floor I lie on,
or burn cool strips into the staring sight
so that they are the shape I close my eye on,
still shining underneath the eyelid, fixed
into my optic pit, a mesh which sticks

or whose rough plate upon the sash-bars lets
strong clouds, when they a little shift, reveal
a blaze of sunlight whose refraction gets
into each hissing engine, so the peal
of steam and light is like the set curvets
of that banked power which drives an inner wheel
as though the majesty of a machine
were something real, or could just be seen;

or the vast picture window frames a chunk
of lake Luzern, while to the lit interior
Luzern lights on the smoky glass when sunk
into the surface of the free irregular
low coffee table, as a pot plant shrunk
by the low ceiling mocks the placed exterior
whose single line of distant mountain drops
to fertile vallies from the snowy tops :

these just play off the standard lamp, whose shade
waits in a corner, & the carpet's grey
sounds the most neutral tone that could be made
showing the afternoon the sun's long way
through to the fireplace where there is displayed
a little sculpture settled there to say
freedom & openness find here their sign.
You gone theodicies of purest line!

The *D'Humysystem*! the swift-folded floors
packed with black oblongs in the rain-filled sky!
Gentle diagonals, your white tower soars
only to mid-height, as it would not try
outmastering the past : which, now, is yours,
in that your disregarded substance stands where I
may wish to saunter, yet I none the less
must not go freely, find each inch confess

combusted energies which might knock flat
who wants the exit kiosk : that dark chink
holds in its centre what divides just that
tarmac of access : you can barely blink
before its sharp edge curves left, as a bat
might be spat out before its ear might think
how not to hit the concrete, lined with neon
to tell free citizens each is its peon.

It is that uninhabitable rock
which makes, of each metropolis, reversion
of those first cells which flowered in the rock,
making, of bitter stone, life's own diversion,
so that life clustered in the sand-scarred rock
of which this car-park is the sheer inversion :
the desert to a city, then, but, here,
the city builds unceasingly to sheer

inoperable blocks, the frozen face
counter-prosopographically set
in blank refusal of each wheel-found place :
the *Dollyprinzip*, the close nestlings met
in lonely parodies of home. No trace
of love & obligation may be met
in this tall stack whose every car is ranked
like assets sleeping where they must be banked.

Moon, who still visits phosphorescent nights,
why do you shine upon these hosts of lighting?
Stars who conceal yourselves behind those lights,
may you be found beneath their shining writing?
Cloud and rain, cover, mist, return all rights
to their first owners, so the unexciting
breath of night air still brush a reeling cheek,
lungs know their choked strength from this feeling weak!

The streets are full of outposts and redoubts.
A concrete island makes its road a stream;
a lit booth fixed among the rapid shouts
of powered vehicles; the street name DREAM;
a bridge, a sidewalk; ineffectual spouts
from public fountains : these are the machine;
these are the public apparatus striving
in proxy apparitions, what's called thriving.

This perfect loneliness, the stone temptation.
All its swept acres speak of human love
as something spent already, so the nation
stores its whole fund of care, till one above
should come to ratify. Disincarnation
unfleshes each rock into mock of love
which lets me walk out & at last just wander
in total licence through the whole grey yonder

as if a leaf or any floating thing
relayed me from appearance to appearance :
as if the mere noise of a word I sing
conveyed me to perpetual disappearance :
as if the sure troths plighted on a ring
were stacked up in a warehouse there for clearance :
these exultations of continuous lack
lock me by link and link to not go back;

I am back anyway. My blind ear listens
out for the least sound of a silver bell :
I watch the rain where each drop stops & glistens
as though each were the single idiomel
borne by prosomia, where no one listens.
The tetramorphic seraphim expel
me without ceasing from the counter-garden
lest irreversibly wrong set and harden

barring the gate to lawful fruits & flowers.
I do in thought attain those longing paths :
I walk in truth where the refreshing showers
gently subject me to these healing baths
& lead me to reanimating bowers
or in the winter to these chosen hearths,
teaching my body to take thought aright,
my soul which has desired thee in the night.

Εὐσπλαγχνίσθητι! I make my own
this skeleton of music in the words :
I let its sinaitic ancient bone
leap in my remnants, as foretelling birds
break up in song the self-preserving stone
or lift their microtones from fifths & thirds
that this long night's kathisma stand up straight
while I sit here in silence and just wait.

The burning bush is here : its microfilm
bears the scratched fact-sheet just below the summit.
I leave each fragment in a broken kiln.
None ever cools : no frost can overcome it,
since, when the acetate on each lost film
moulders and turns, those blossoms which become it
flower irrefutably, and let their text
explode in this world from the shining next.

The hierosolymitan, the psalter
intercalating with a secret thought
each round of psalmody, as each might alter
just with one mind-event the path it sought
or this unheard idea let no foot falter
treading its radiance in each next ought
to bring me simply to this same midnight
where I sit still awaiting real light.

I love my enemy : the motorways
knot themselves freely into free designs
which from the mountain in a perfect blaze
rage out in creams and colours like the signs
of unimaginable grandeur, haze
of unexampled wealth whose wheeling lines
burn on the black land their incessant clamour
or mirror image of satanic glamour

whose mask is function, but whose real power
calls through the night like an apotropaic
pattern of talismans, the witching hour
of modern travel, or the top archaic
glass-cast mimesis, the unliving flower
blossomed and blossomed to this fixed mosaic
set in the valley floor, where each bright car
is just the circumambulating star

pursuing its free purpose to the next
free filling station. Shining in the night,
these little archipelagoes, pretext
for counters, shelves, of incandescent white,
hymn out continuously neon text
which each lit dot treats like the source of light,
a little touch to tarry in the black
or linger fondly over each chocked stack

and to select some one companion candy
to go with it into the soul's Nevada :
yip with exhilarants, as night paints sandy
wastes its one colour, while I must look harder
straight at the road ahead. It's dandy.
I crush pneumatically the intifada
of cowering tarmacs, as my jet black truck
converts this fallenness to just my luck,

then turns the other fist. I love too much :
transcendence pictures that remembered drive
without the roof-struts propping up the hutch
in failing nylon, since each thought would skive
off from the stones of Reno, blank back such
with all their bonded polymers in live
killings of every molecule which speaks
what plastics had to die to feed those peaks.

The thick sky fills with dread; the clouds drive down
the crushed streets steadily, & each forced breath
comes each time harder, till the little town
chokes at each vent, forgets its very clef
of worked polyphonies, and just sinks down
into persistence of unyielding death
which I live now, in this unceasing room
where all those unappeasing spirits whom

I suck each breath from, stop my mouth with coins,
and in the centre of remembered pain
feel where each necessary sorrow joins
and interlocks remainderlessly : pain
repeats unvaryingly, nor disjoins
its seamless iterations, its same pain
from every part of my receiving limbs.
Quick terror issues in believing hymns

sprung from this wordless quiddity, whose inch
thickens and thickens in its stuck refrains
where every time I would get up or flinch
the stuff won't budge, but patiently explains
I must await a trolley or a winch
to haul me off or upright. It disdains
whatever could be thought about it, throbs
in self-same ignorance of threats and sobs.

Let it come down; it will do anyway;
that round optative adds a little strum
to what just breaks upon me when the day
may not be countermanded, & I come
up to the surface drowned, as who should say
he makes the dawn by this twitch of his thumb,
moves tides with eyelids, lips command the moons,
or men and nations with his ten-step tunes.

So at the bottom of unhappiness
I often find my hands will make a sign
crossing in front of me, as though no less
than instruments unable to resign
their never efficacity, or rest
until this little gesture, this design
fill all the air before them with compulsion
obsessed with rescue, mastery, revulsion :

as though these crossings could repeal one woe
or wash it painlessly into the ocean :
as though hand over hand might make it go
or dissipate it to an empty notion :
as though each finger's quiver were to know
how to reverse fixated wrong devotion :
so in the street I semaphore distress
or thus in public secretly confess.

The broke-rebuilded temple : each shook face,
be trembling opposite to skulking dog
& dog dog-auditors, dog-tweets! One place
on my rebellious body burns king log
& fills by quaking with redundant grace :
restore the song-stock, fund the mystagog!
Silver and gold sequestered from the spring,
let standing waters blossom, let each thing

still stand transfigured in its own persistence
nor send a proxy to the copper drop!
Let each fixed proper be its own resistance,
each collect gather from the back and top!
From mouth to mouth, the kiss of gripped existence,
from hand to hand that thought which never stops
but builds incessantly in demolitions,
brings all true concepts to correct volitions.

Stones live reluctantly : each chip is hewn
into this edifice of thinking blocks
whose lapidary settings might untune
with stone-felt staffs, stone steps, the sounding box
which once a hundred years emits a tune
heard by one ear till it snaps shut and locks
its needful melodies away for ever
which are recovered when I thus dissever

line from prose line, word's grown nail from the flesh.
This puts the colour in the moor's new heather,
lets the grain leap out from the wheat you thresh;
strips the first letter from despairing Never,
rends the false screen to let the true and fresh
veil veil your cashless mystery forever,
opens the graves to let the dead men thank,
live workers sing down, the demolished bank.

Each true disaster sees another star
rise from its ashes, since the broken church
is first the church then when its ruins are
ruins of ruins, and the worm's research
is to find out those rubbles whose bits are
codes of the future, where the bee's sweet search
reports at length, in lieu of unpaid tax,
to the state's ruins, honey, gold & wax.

Here at the window I may calmly drink
line after line of air. This earth's true task :
choose what is given, and then make it think
its gifts back better than the work they ask.
Each verse redeems me from the withheld blink
of that face melded to its own stuck mask
which immemorially stares and stares
into my bashed one back, which grins & bears

the disobeyed instruction to enjoy
the unit maximum, the quantity :
the lidless eye which wishes to destroy
each minuscule equivocation, be
the sightless lens admitting each known joy
only so far as instantaneously
it may be sent down to the silical
reserves, sump, hoard, the still-killed miracle.

Instead I let this inch of freezing air
travel across my face : it is the news
of what reanimates my disrepair
so that, once this has visited, I choose
more really, in that the constant glare
of choice's abstract million trips a fuse,
letting reflection breathe once more in darkness
thought's recollection in its viewless fastness.

Come to me now : now sinks the whole false star.
Come to be near me, since the whole night now
invests and treads me, and the last lights are
dimmed to invisible remainders : now
the bright hour sleeps, and the unresting car
is parked in silence : O my love, come now,
now when the deep dark wraps its best of black
round each wrong consciousness of mutual lack.

This air comes trembling : like the only sound
known in this room tonight, its unforced tremor
configures images of underground
echoes of music, like that written stemma
which must be lost in order to be found
or whose thought tightens to some one dilemma :
sated with wrong, or stuffed with fat rejection,
make Dante's journey in the wrong direction.

It is almost impossible to breathe.
The globe's gross total presses on my chest
as though it were prohibited to leave
one single thing out of account, or rest
permitted only to who shall conceive
all persons simultaneously. The best
stops off my lung with its continuous block.
I long to harden, dry, die, set like rock.

It is as though the view from outer space
were perfect vision, & each non-duration
were to be multiplied by each non-place
to make a graven image of the nation
or real existence were at once disgrace
delivering to proper execration
each little deviation from the blank
suit of self-cancelling, the thankless tank.

Count back the realm of numbers : make my cell
their sounding abacus, until each sum
come back in pitches, & the debt's clear bell
ring down this pantomime, so I may come
sheer from that zero whose results can't tell
a single thing about the world. Strike dumb
loquacious ciphers & their vacant cash;
save me from stiff cremations, hell's lived ash.

So the same rhythm which repels my pain
is what I think with in unsleeping night.
The same held melody which salves again
wakes Adam's apple from its key-struck blight.
So my reluctant gulp, my trained refrain
tells the taught throat at once to stand upright.
Throat, tune, pulse, apple, know your proper name;
so you may dapple what would really blame

persisting life. I wander now in thought;
I drift off over to the riverside;
I let my book drop; I forget what ought
to redirect each instant to denied
experience, my willing soul : thought's fort
sorts its poor remnants on the burnt inside,
while I just sit here staring into space.
I am that piece which may not leave its place.

Fixed on the inside of the feeling eye
one mark besets each temple I behold :
each is built up into the top of high
faith and assertion, each fills up its cold
tunnels and galleries with gaps where I
roam without ceasing in the still unsold
centre of quietness, the set kept zone,
where each with all must always walk alone.

A fire refines me when it burns me down.
Which incombustible reserve retains
one single quality, which little frown
sends entire continents of my remains
up in blank gases? which pretended crown
sits on these ashes? which deferred refrains?
Burnt & burnt up into the best excess
I would restore the palaces of less.

The year needs set gaps : so this longest night
knows its quick shipwrecks & repeat collapses.
The turning earth persuades eternal light
to fall in seasons, whose reverted apses
cease & return in cycles, as though right
live off subjunctives & their held perhapses
without which we were saved into sclerosis
of instantaneous apotheosis.

One night's continuous terror is a stroke
scissoring certainty of mineness : what
scatters my known path like a line of coke
sent to the four winds by one breath, leaves shot
my coat of defaults, or with one light joke
alters each circumstance, each swash & jot
I had thought written through my bones in steel
and makes them what I happened, once, to feel,

this same revenging quantum helps me limp
back to this other line, the head's lent measure,
hums back the tune whose singers never skimp
their shared assistance, poverty's poor treasure :
I skip up quickly with an unclipped imp
tripping with inexterminable pleasure,
living more wholly when more dispossessed,
more quite sustained as less known or caressed.

How many years is it since this thin arm
knew on its field of skin one human touch?
I stiffen instantly, since one fixed charm
has me in quarantine, commanded such
that any contact might release dire harm
depopulating nations. Brain's dumb hutch
hoards in those places it at once suppresses
its made-up dairymaids and shepherdesses.

Transverberate my heart! these cardiac
unfetterings disperse through every part
up from my toenails to my breast & back
reanimating by this stroke of art
sectors I had thought sent down to the black
since the refrain of this transfixing dart
feasts with the opposite of blank arrest
my fast-bound body to this perfect rest.

Come suddenly, because my stock of fats
is trimmed & ready : I maintain all night
my dim lamp flickering in these damp flats
as though it could secure me from the fright
I must know when you come. Magnificats
make up my timekeeping until the light
shall break upon me, and I may go down
from this fixed pillar to the street & town.

Believe this writing rather than my cries
whenever I shall wish to go on living.
Inside each head there is a crucified
flesh of kept longings, mesh of unforgiving
furies latched on to their displaced devised
dying immortally. Cash ends up giving
its whole sold pyramid as the machine
failing to carry me beyond the screen :

this ink stands for me like the written proxy
retaining with its delible notations
each free leap whose recovered orthodoxy
lets doctrine lift it, while the wrong flotations
disperse in paper, when its thought-up doxy
patches its matter out of misquotations.
I walk instead inside that floated voice
whose necessary knowledge must rejoice.

The teeth of lions may not thresh the corn
more swiftly than I transit through the mill.
Issue in nourishments, since all lost scorn
flies off like chaff, & the remaining will,
one grain of incense, one insisting thorn,
may with its silent action swiftly fill
each limb's quick motors with those lively notions,
inert recumbents with benign commotions.

My thought's Whit Tuesday, brain's flipped Echternach.
I bound and skip in thought along the line
chalked out for three steps forward and two back,
five steps, to move up one, since, by design,
we creep directly to the source of lack
or indirectly to the shining sign :
so as I lie here sleeplessly, obsession
plots each sweet jump of this divine procession.

My head immediately fills with light
here in this darkness where before the dawn
my blind eye dazzles at its proper sight,
my garment mended as if never worn.
I am illuminated. As the night
deepens & blackens still into the torn
black on black fabric of light's disparition,
I burn continuously from this first ignition.

I turn the little figurine away
whenever I cannot endure to face it.
When, at the close of work's estranged sold day,
each lack demands that I at once replace it
with images whose colour seems to say
I might know happiness while I deface it
I must then turn the tin man suffering
round to the window, where he sees each thing

pass in the street, but nothing in the room.
I beg this sentinel to watch for me
now that I am protected by the gloom,
rapt in each false thought, wishing just to be
inexorably made that one to whom
delightful dissolutions come & free
each requisitioned nerve to speak and tingle,
each once-collectivized thought curve to single

vaults and saltations in the various sky.
Stand then and face the street when I do wrong,
but, when I need you, come, since then all my
devices and desires run out : my song
squeaks its apologies, croaks, grunts, and I
would be unable to avoid the long
dinner of millinery, brought up flat
against the day I have to eat my hat.

These chimes and echoes form the long relay
postponing that intolerable minute
when I should not be able to delay
sight of my face and all the crimes hid in it :
so the quick rhapsode stitches up all stray
fact-calques and formulas, where who would bin it
must stare down total knowledge of his error,
continuous inobviable terror.

One to another, they blot out this pain
as though they were the opposite of torches
lit on the summits in a fiery chain
to warn of armies; while each brand leaves scorches,
these rhyme-denials let the resting brain
suspend emergencies, clear airy porches
where normal service always is resumed
whatever headwear has to be consumed.

These linked clips make a rhythm where I may
relent to undirected recollection.
These brief sweet intervals can let me say
in wordless periods how steep dejection
still may not capture all there is to say
since even touch may at its own election
recall the very texture of one kind
caress or kiss, a cheek's or lip's felt mind.

No such event may ever be narrated.
Its hidden qualities refuse expulsion
just as some angels will not be created
but hold their radiance in fixed compulsion
not to appear & not to be related :
they are the spirits of a lit repulsion
from diminution in this field of stories
or earth's dilution of their groundless glories.

Then any circumstantial detail which
I seek to note, from these resistances,
is the broke parts of it, the helpless kitsch
wanting to versify existences
or scratch in dactyls this ten-fingered itch
yet at the same time paint persistences
of shade's protagonists, their thoughts and actions,
those still personified & lived redactions.

You pass so high above the sun that I
may barely contemplate your rising track.
As it sets there, you leap beyond the sky,
leaving this left earth to return to black.
I am abandoned : I go blank in my
each bereft organ, as I must tread back
these steps past the shut kiosk in the rain,
assured that one day you will come again,

so that the cycle of abandonments
works up fierce ecstasies in every minute.
Each hole gets covered, each thick tear or rent
has each some picture of delight stuffed in it.
Each atom shrivels from the place it meant.
Each pixel swivels. I may not begin it
except I shut down every lost device
& self-congeal into this feeling ice.

Then these returns are not the labyrinth
willing its involution, may not fold
event upon event, as plinth on plinth,
to let me disappear, as though some old
root of unextirpated terebinth
might at its flower bespeak a buried gold
still to be quarried from the central earth.
I speak continuing refrains of dearth

since, when I stare up to the dark grey ceiling
I may not see those patterns which collect
around the power cable : so blind feeling
must now be felt blind, nor may I reflect
one flake of paint back on the wall whose peeling
layers abandon it, and then elect
descent, decay, & then at last collection
in scattered patches. I wish disconnection

which could resolve me into final stones :
I may not build a monument, so set
here into fixity, when stubborn bones
refuse to leave their place, & will not let
one lucky offer free them, but set tones
here like an auditory statue, met
at any hour in place of their dead author
who keeps on writing thanks to matchless torpor

which disallows cessation. I crave ink
kept in a bottle to refresh the page
as though the little scritches that I think
were black refreshments which might here assuage
long desiccations, or the paper drink
quick from each gesture the reverse of rage
yet with all frenzy's passionate exactness
where white is severed by its sinking blackness,

whereas this night's sheet is the opposite
since constellations & their maps of white
chart in its gulf with their imagined lit
figures & ciphers what I may not write
there in the sky which slides away from it
before with any particle of bright
fire or burnt artifice I might just mark
one fugitive appeal into the dark.

Unconquerable as the sparks that shine
out from tried metal in the sunless black
I skulk down backwards to what would be mine
& which I corner from imagined lack.
I slump, revert, I stumble, blurt : each line
must from this source of failing be dragged back
like the dead man who stands at last upright
first when he stiffens into lifeless night.

The heart fills up with motor oil : each crime
commissioned for me blocks one passage there.
Its hurt intelligence recedes each time
unkindness triumphs in that engine, where
blood's habits may become the very clime
propitious or disastrous to that care
which lets me notice any thing at all
or turns my face forever to the wall.

Eleven years I stared into the map
of wasted luxuries upon the font.
Eleven years I let the salving tap
run out barbiturates into blocked want
and sucked eleven years upon the pap
whose anaesthetic was my symbiont
drinking prosthetically each least cell
from those clenched lips which latched themselves too well

on to its tube, the opposite of milk.
Eleven years I gripped its little phones
into my blocked ear, while this counter-milk
burned & assuaged with its appeasing tones
each single minute, as a nylon silk
might line my lungs or hollow out my bones
until the whole corpse were a vibrant mankin
fit to take orders or to build a bank in.

Eleven years I would not breathe the air
or let another living being touch me.
Eleven years of fancying despair
whose brilliant spirits still implore and clutch me.
Eleven years of blocking disrepair
into that simulacrum which might hutch me
happy as beasts inside my work and fodder
where any real perception must seem odder

than this lived nothing of the cash-strapped clock.
Release me, raise me, burn me, break and bear
your still-rung burden up against the block
which would protect investments of despair
and with eleven years stick down the lock
leaving me glued in stupid pleasure there
or seal cupidities into this nation,
forever fending off decompensation.

Eleven years connected to the drip
inserted in each atom of my skin :
eleven years of longing for the skip
or any vile container which might bin
these irrepressible remains which trip
up like the wrong root of incarnate sin :
eleven and eleven and eleven,
even these numbers with your odd lost heaven!

I self-assimilate these mechanisms.
What I might use, I make my element
until it squirms & wriggles, organism
almost of living diodes, or then sent
to desecrate all temples, heal all schisms
into the broad church of forgetting, meant
continuators of resistless hell.
We go down silently, & know too well

in each case just that part we must erase.
Now from blank jelly sight's surviving organs
look out in terror; from its nights & days
immortal hearing tears its choking portions
and the false tongue stumps up its glut of praise
for the cash-totals, since those happy gorgons
stare in commandment from each speaking stone
ten laws of self-selection, cells' tenth throne.

Immortal speaking, break the vegetated
tooth, tongues & palate! now, you flesh-sent spirit,
sing fifty alphabets to faux-belated
unsciences of stuffs! A broken spirit
breaks carapaces which incarcerated
this suffering-desiring-thinking spirit
in extrajections of its long sweet night,
the wrong beside itself as fallen light,

so that I rest at last in perfect dark.
I let all striving drop; I merely breathe
this air for nothing, and make no remark
if not to notice how the spent breath leaves
refreshed lungs happy for the happy lark
never to come with sweet song which bereaves
me of continual night whose lovely blacks
keep all deep colours in their viewless tracks.

The night treads onward to week thirty-four.
The Grand Canal south-east of Babylon
still bears its captives south : those waters pour
resistlessly into the ocean, gone
out to that destination whence no more
they may return. I am born out upon
immensities of fossils burning down
each last seclusion, till the fire come round

into the very substance of my sensing.
It burns with signals : every little cell
flares with some symbol, fragranceless, incensing
that no part of the body may be well
spared its continuous scouring and recensing
because this money longs to eat & sell
all that plays dead, shuts up, or just lies quiet
in order not to make up its cash-diet.

Non-jurors doggo in the soviet
are set down in its pleistocene, or dumped
along compartments of forgetting, met
in masks contorted where their faces slumped
into defeats whose worst of worst waits yet
to greet the trashed neck when the bleeding stump
sing of a kingless cash across the water
& the succession fall on Lenin's daughter.

So the procession of deleted queens
makes its slow progress down into the earth.
My heart leaps up into a star which means
the counter-kingdom of immortal mirth
merely declining these repeated scenes,
my money's parody of growth, of birth,
the quenchless agony of undead buds
breaking detergents into tide-split suds.

All that is solid melts, not into air,
but chlorofluorocarbons and dioxins :
each dissolution sequestrates its fair
share of Christ's assets to produce more toxins :
I walk in freedom to just anywhere
letting the clangours of combusting tocsins
strike on this impotent and resting ear
in order that I may know just which fear

I am to listen out for in the night.
Not every paranoia is an angel.
Yet each sparse car arriving in the night
seems to bring messages, as any angel
encountered in the middle of the night
sits me bolt upright in the bed. An angel
is what can grip you by the chest and neck
or help you irretrievably to wreck

your plans and wishes, your entire lost scheme.
So from these terrible dominions song
squeals like an aircraft, or emits a scream
whose arias squeak upwards to the wrong
top note of punishment, the day's one theme
of life's ejection and its void or long
sober self-sale into the sticky treat
which every miserable mouth must eat.

Now the whole series of them are convened
in terror and in judgement round my bed.
Their adorations strike my unredeemed
ear; they reverberate along my head.
Their antiphons and anthems are not dreamed :
I know this instant of the purest dread
not as a metaphor, a tune or trope,
but in the very letter on the rope.

From the four quarters of the sleeping earth
they must denounce my vacancies and blurs.
Immortal vision in their keen-eyed mirth
opens me gently, as a scalpel stirs
the feeling surface of the skin, or birth
wakes the excruciated infant's first
cry of deaf lack, its utter need and terror,
the first sweet treble in its song of error.

Inside this room it is as though the cries
of every baby ever born were brought
to break that carapace of honest lies
in which I snuggle like the last best fort :
my each last argument, ditch where last dies
life's endless labour of deferring thought
until tomorrow, which believing sink
chokes on detritus, that it need not think.

I am cut down into continuous
remorses and remorseless reckoning :
I wake into this discontinuous
series of punctures, as if each last thing
must cleave my skin, or, non-continuous,
let hid bones kiss the air. My wounds must sing,
since they all open when my sewn mouth closes,
hope to commemorate the truth with roses.

It is as though this tiniest device
alone releases me through true constraint
to let thaw one block in the brain's kept ice,
unlock one cell, permit one thought to paint
one recollected real through super-nice
interextricable or clocked restraint :
so rhyme's dumb echo lifts the living word
down from its purgatories of inferred

continuous torment into tenderness.
Care for the dead in song : know, know the tunes.
Let those departed tear my throat no less
than uncreated splendour which oppugns
each immemorial melody. Caress
their cold remains with longing : good grief swoons
into incessant wishes and petition
for each dead soul to know its repetition

into insuperable happiness.
I wait to be torn up : each crawling second
ratchets desire one notch along its guess
at coming pain, until each creak is reckoned
down in the listening centre. I confess
my wish to go to where I still am beckoned
into impenetrable realms of light
whose worldly negative is this long night.

I wear my body closer than a stone.
No gem is brighter than its inner optic
flooding with colours all the monochrome
pandisidealized or nonsynoptic
city of dire ejections. I alone
may not be captured by hell's spelt panoptic.
We are each one of us composed of life
in hidden substance and vivacious strife.

The bright defunct return me to the lip
of what I would abolish or destroy
each time I turn back, or would simply skip
each necessary step. Without alloy
they bring true metals from those earths which grip
the subterranean remains of joy
firmly into that incandescent past
which burns down in me to the very last.

There where my longing for oblivion runs
I am ignited into painful waking :
where each sad atom of my thinking shuns
the new day's task of yet again remaking
the same jet spring from rock, the keen dead come
accompanying me, nor once forsaking,
in zealous care for me, my creeping track
backwards and forwards down into the black.

They suffer for me on the folding slope
where woes rain down from the corroded sky :
they think inside me, speak, repeat & hope
when I sink back disjected, or when I
just want to give myself enough strong rope
or wish to taste that second when I die.
Those souls in agony for whom I pray
bear and foresuffer me into the day.

I shall be opened like the seventh seal
so that each kufiq written on my spleen
may self-unravel, and its lines reveal
the various account of what I mean
until that exhumation when I peel
my thousand skins into the kerosene,
dead set on necessary immolations
of all death's presents, bribes, and consolations.

Then you shall read me like an open book.
Each mark of folly on my back and chest
shall from the inside of the body look
reversed into a cipher of the best
denoting contours of the tune it took
until it should by force of forethought wrest
saints to their index, angels to their list,
faithful departed to their sigla, kissed

with ink's quick tokens, and returned to stand
at the ten edges of recorded time.
My recollection inundates the land,
leaving the names upon each hill I climb,
stuck to each river, fixture, bridge, road, and
making the map this dictionary of rhyme
calling the dead to bury once again
their dead protectors in the freezing rain.

I walk out in imagination now
far from this bed, this city, and this room :
I tread those crests of limestones which endow
each sheltered settlement with stone. To whom
all this is given, when, where, why and how,
I answer like lights written in the gloom
with just this series of the toponyms
fixed to a landscape like the fossil hymns

whose stony phonemes concentrate the loss
worked up by strenuous forgetting. This
makes of each line mind-trodden its own cost,
bought with those unstamped metals which must miss
their proper vocables, clink spirit-tossed
in the cash vacuum. I come back to this :
that whole drowned atlas of celestial places
known as the sheer names spoken from our faces.

I walk in thought towards this earthly vision.
The very stones repeat to me their names
as though those mouthlings were the sweet division
letting them stand there, or the silent claims
to recollect each marginal elision
by which each wheel unthinkingly defames
in false immediacy every stone
it triumphs over with a howling drone

the driver never hears. The stones rise up :
their centuries contract into a minute.
The rivers drain into a single cup;
the wolds and scarps fold under, through and in it :
each letter speaks its name, each is bound up
into that stroke which could again begin it;
towns, cities, villages, must learn to stay
the names of paradise in common day.

In little imitations of the light
the darkness flickers, and inside my head
hallucinated stars are put to flight :
it is that voluntary on sheer dread
whose crackle of magnesium tears night
into a myriad scintillations fled
where each reflecting and resounding angle
sets to return that light and sound they mangle

until this head might be the thinking bone
racked by its artworks : the Cavaillé-Coll
of cracked part-resonable skull, the phone
calling with tremolos or fulgurant doll
whose rapid descants know the very tone
of the last day when all the mountains roll
down to the ocean, and the rent earth knows
its dissolution, as the cross one rose.

I make it up from what is all around me :
darkness, invisibility, and pain.
I take my bed up from the place which found me
nailed to the spot as if no drop of rain
must ever brush my face, as if, around me,
each single thing forever must remain
identical and dead until the end,
each turn a cold face to its speaking friend.

Then every sound which falls into this room
comes through the window like the news of life.
Each like a light wakes noises in the gloom
or enters wet, because its rain-soaked life
may be detected by the one for whom
this inner ear may listen to the life :
infinitesimally striking hammer
retrieving real things from their sign-chimed glamour.

A brake disc or a dropped coin in the street
has each its proper clavichord, its scale
of audibles, in whose restored complete
brush at the tympanum, I never fail
to be revived. Reality, replete
with every detail, batter, break, assail
this tender prison, scatter, take for dead
this rented flat of the defended head!

God's acre in the thorax, where there grow
just those swift cankers whose true choking trees
blossom in horror, just until I show
their signals at my dumbstruck vertices :
these eyes speak panic, while the mouth must go
down at the edges, study how to please
the struck brain falling at one side which drops
slack face-collapses from my long lost tops.

Bury redempted organs in my chest.
I breathe around them, as a whistle gets
its tune from that hole in between the rest
of smashed enamels, where the broke tooth lets
airs & sweet melodies escape. My vest
lifts and drops back; my wheezing breast-box vets
each gulp of fuel with its blocked pneumatic
predisinflators when the automatic

has to learn how to do the whole damned thing
from the beginning, when the breathless coral
gathers and hardens in the lung : so, sing
from these shrubbed windpipes your austerest moral
note of subtraction! Let the stripped lines bring
prose sense alone to the discoloured laurel
and verse print only its intended notes
spoken in figureless reserve which floats

thought's silent melody along the page.
In paradisum, to the cemetery;
but, *dies irae*, when projected rage
I would propitiate, yet may not vary,
nor by one little inch at all assuage,
offers to bear me down : I call on Mary,
hail holy molies in a helpless panic
but get no other than the same satanic

answer of ice, my own long coldness back.
All those I passed in silence, to my face
tell me : you froze, you burnt me, turned your back
on this unintermittent wrong : now grace
should get you out of it, should take you back
just with a shrug and kiss, repair disgrace
just in a twinkling, and let's get along?
You are to be forgiven for a song?

No; know instead precisely how it feels
to know untarnished insignificance,
coupled with matchless pain which leaps & reels
hot in each atom : copy up that dance
danced by the leper whose exclusion keels
each limb he has to wrongwards. It's your chance
at last to find out what you did and acted,
to pay smack-taxes you yourself exacted.

The seven last plagues in the seven bowls
are held by seven angels. To my lips
each now advances with tormented souls
each of whom bears the files, receipts, & slips
of cash transactions : each one now controls
one instant of my history, or dips
its look to where I am incinerated.
Now strip me of the wish to be belated.

Stand me up single, so this here and now
knows its primaeval mediations, sent
through the whole anamnetic spiral : bow
each upright bone then back into the bent
recursiveness of spirit, so that how
I may get up is only by the lent
action and vigilance of all the dead
recurring twice a second in my head.

I am commanded to continuate
that without which I should at once subside
into prosthesis of the counter-state :
the offshore fuck club, hoarded & denied
theft from collective trust, the lied outside
which leverages from the thought of late
vile depredations on the hills and pastures
& men who work them for their proxy masters.

Then only by this exercise in song
may I at all produce one little break
in webbed disownings, or at all prolong
a thought from one breath to the next I take
without receiving cash for it : the wrong
blipped recognitions, which I here forsake
into forgottenness whose only flaw
is that one individual whose more

determined, patient, and untiring care
will tread these tundras one line at a time
as though her wish were for the crust to melt
and there begin again beneath the ice
a human word of greeting whose device
need not eclipse a face, but bring news spelt
with unfeigned *Heiterkeit*, as if its clime
had known one slip into the springtime there :

so when I round the corner and I see
in front of me one long procession pass
of all those marching, and one friend hails me,
I momentarily forget to class
this moment as false solidarity
but march instead myself to where amass
the plural human for one hour persuaded
that all share all need even in degraded

professions, cadres, sects and shut divisions.
It is as though we were to be alive
first as together when the flag envisions
some wrong bright rubric under which can thrive
suspension of our doubts and quick revisions,
and, then, as though this moment's life should drive
down to the place where all glass must be broken
to say iconoclasm is the woken

face of rough justice & the smashing fun
releasing human labour into sprinkles
of shattered images where shards catch sun
and ring the pavement with beheaded tinkles :
let it come down into the morning sun :
deface the father, since his plaster wrinkles
must be stormed through into the vacant towers
wracked with a wish to slash the very hours.

Now watch us fall apart : one cardboard flap
flops to the river, and I must disperse
appeasedly to where a little trap
holds my small fortunes. Yes, it can get worse.
It can get colder : so I shrink, I wrap
my coat around me, while I note in verse
the lift & swoop & then the blank deflations
of all these real & real recalled elations.

If no one atom of the city can
forever be reversed, the damage sticks
inside each wish to mend it : when I ran
right down the street as if hot blows or licks
could break through coldness to a better man,
one cold ferocity, one rill of Styx
slept in my blood, so that all fight not mental
turned out to be not just, just instrumental.

Then must these plastic panels and their splits
in brilliant primaries across the grey
make part of my necessity? Lorn chits
slip down out of my hand : must then glad day
forever now be locked, because the pits
exist already, & the earth's wounds say
they are the vulnerated real, the true
all-irreversible reply to who

would think of Sion when the morning light
scatters the shut face of the sleeping earth,
breaking to colour & to wakening sight
roof, street, hill, valley, warehouse, garage, firth?
Must what has happened be forever right
because it happened, & must ancient mirth
strap the long yoke of prose into its face
forced to strip nature of her single grace?

Must every ring-pull on the bloody road
still self-personify *raison d'état*?
Must each trick symbol, each quick sign corrode
trust at the double, roll the round earth flat?
Must I still seal my eyes up, overload
my stuck tongue with its decalogue of chat?
Must each worse step forever and forever
be sweetly tucked up in the box marked Never?

You must put on each atom to be healed.
Two wills, two natures : else there would still be
some hair or fingernail whose sheer repealed
stuff were discarded. To the human sea
you came down drenched then & at once unsealed
each stopped-up chamber, as though each must be
at once transfigured, and your single face
illuminate itself at every place

in twofold charity. I see you now
in my reviled mind's eye : as though invisible
limitless love might none the less allow
nocturnal hiddennesses to take visible
face so that none might fairly disavow
good's countenance. This indivisible
good face demands division of its natures,
as longing for it animates its creatures.

Impermanent as these eternal inks
I watch your gestures for a mark of light
which to the one who waits, attends and thinks
must surely come at last, although no bright
seraph or herald decorate its brinks
nor touch my mouth, yet as day follows night
I cannot but be finished off in time
leaving these coal-black characters to shine

for me until they be erased or burnt.
The florilegium against monothelite
doctrine locks blossoms to the thoughts they learnt
so that the theory of correct delight
may never be dispersed by some unearnt
fault in the person, blot or blur which might
meld your two natures and thus break your face
into the wrong parts of a blank disgrace :

so that instead you may at last inhabit
every lost part of me, from teeth and nails
to gone surmises the sunk brain must rabbit
when the unconscious from itself derails
itself's long wish into a thoughtless habit
or the hand falters and the foot just fails
so that I crash, fall, fold, collapse and stumble
returning limbs to their first mingled jumble.

You had to know the long calcification
of heart and liver, lungs and throat and spleen :
yours was the quiver of the quick vibration
felt up the spine whenever the serene
instant of verse should colour a carnation
in the beginning when the word I mean
sing, twist & hurtle through the page of air
to plant ideas in the brain where there

grow all these melodies of logos, rapt
with reason's reasons in electric leaps,
so that the thought in which a tune is wrapped
lifts and proliferates until it keeps
an indestructible correction trapped
in fifty million pounds of tissue, steeps
the recapitulated song in heads
like winter pips in snow-curated beds.

So locusts, crocodiles & sex for one
could not be tolerated as the smallest part
of your blest limbs, since his pure soul must shun
repulsive insects, & protect your heart
from all contaminations. Like the sun :
he must take incarnation for that art
which makes your real body out of stars
nor ever stuffs with excrements what mars

what he supposes incorruptible
until the very end. What Marcion
considered a disgrace, the risible
worm eating lumps out of the dead & gone
body of skin, to me is visible
flesh of salvation whose demise folds on
to just that sacrament by which I know
I am alive and kicking even though

continuous revolutions of the wheel
plead & cajole me to identify
my total substance with what cannot feel
or think one instant : so when you and I
kiss here it is that rose-cross of the real
suffered, desired and thought without a why
more prenarrated than this lifelong weaning,
this ineradicable sea of meaning.

In utter darkness this persisting sense
confirms its apophatic feints and shrinkings :
it swells, recedes, dilates : it is one dense
resisting mass of fears, joys, pains, deep drinkings
of its impressional returns, intense
rhythm of night-veiled passions, wishes, thinkings :
I may not distance it however hard I jam it
through the third person, since I simply am it.

So the revoked close of my blocked interior
is what you prise apart : sweet wood, sweet nails,
ping to the self-ejecting blank exterior
its own flat affects, since your ship now sails
into Jerusalem where no whit wearier
I fly the standard where the sun still fails
to rise tomorrow morning for the sceptic
letting those syllogisms too dyspeptic

to swallow wonders eat their own chopped logic.
The cut off right hand and the torn out eye
float like reft emblems of their theologic
transfiguration to those organs I
think in the air with : so the mystagogic
disvegetated sense permits the sky
to be the sky and not that troop of gases
it disassembles to whenever masses

of sheer existents would at once usurp
this earth's imperium. I sit and stare
into the darkness round my bed whose work
is set out for me, where the same stuck chair
fixes me out into the blank I shirk.
I must continuously notice there
disturbances of black : as black tracks back
black's swirls and spirals of imperfect lack.

Break the phantasmal body : docetist
panreconnectors wish my life to be
all pixelled spirit in a hub's big list
of switches, pick-ups, points of light whose free
inevitable transits send their hissed
sequence of digits to the still unfree
silical pyramids whose tax evasions
stand on the sand outbraving all persuasions.

Certain impossibles make unsidereal
my shaking face & spiritual gut :
teeth are not stars, nor may I eat ethereal
meals of transparency. I'd like to but
smears of jam butter up the milk-soaked cereal
all the way down to where the law would cut
immaculated leprosies apart
and set its password, the sequestered heart.

My human body knew how to be born.
Its intertextures of injuncted nerves
must in transfigured ignominy scorn
or with a little jink elude, with blessed swerves
escape symbolic regimens which warn
each little muscle to renounce its curves
and settle down now dead into the drive
happy to be released from this alive

work of the anxious soul. I know these stones
rung in my marrow, since the richest treasure
is the most hidden : deep inside my bones
ice cracks to trickles, and one unfree pleasure
rattles & bangs inside me, as who moans
inaudibly to feel the proper measure
re-order scattered thoughts into these lines
of tender sensings & their made designs.

Sense is the soul of soul : my fingers know
each precious square inch of your darkened face.
The soul must sense, or else it could not so
retain implacably each little trace
of nameless detail. Everything must go :
yet every passage brushes by some place
whose name contains just this scent and this tune,
whose letters reconvene these late & soon.

Gratuitously as the rain that falls
I may imagine wine drip from the mountains
even as round me these four hidden walls
were to conceal intarissable fountains
flowing & flowing through this room. What calls
like torrents dropping from the sharpest mountains
into this flowering desert, this fixed cell,
this one room palace of expiring well?

My life is hidden in indifference.
Hour after hour this little city state
knows revolutions, as the heart's pump sends
elations, exclamations, to their fate
in numbed extremities when blood distends
their re-awakened knowledge, yet too late
distributes thoughts to each blocked ward or sector
where each has disavowed the resurrector.

This night's long history will find no chronicle.
Its marches and campaigns belong to dust.
Its proper destiny is one ironical
note in a footnote in a tale of just
what follies shook the comic non-canonical
verse outliers; and then that note will rust,
corrode to nothing, till I am forgotten
most efficaciously into the rotten

persisting landfills west of Belarus.
Then I shall sleep for twenty thousand years.
The sea's quick action can at once unloose
those grains of sand in which a name appears.
Implacably the future will refuse
to know my name, and these long hopes and fears
attain insuperable sleep, inert
there with the rocks no calumny may hurt.

The clock strikes three : the winter's dark
prepares a solitude within the year
as though this night were salted in an ark
lost in an arctic ocean, or my fear
were not to thaw till spring. I mark
each starving feast off on the inner ear :
the lost souls call out like a bird awoken
some hours before the morning can have broken.

It is completely silent in this room.
No word can reach me of your life and fate.
The little inch which opens to the gloom,
down at the bottom where an old tin plate
props up the sash, lets in no breath. For whom,
or what, must this transpire? At what fixed date
is it to end, or must its stone wheel never
cease pulverizing, but just turn for ever?

Bird of the winter night, I cannot not
picture your voice as phosphorescent white.
I know it has no colour, yet may not
prevent the image of one super-bright
or imperceptible quick firework shot
too rapidly to be detained by sight
like that swift spirit who from deepest black
scatters illuminations in her track.

St. Lucy whom I neither hear nor see!
Spring from your non-existence one spirit's spark :
let the elision of that sixth word be
the interval in which your silver barque
slips its fixed moorings, and sink down to me
here in the city of the drowned, the dark
metropolis of all those irretrievably
removed from grace & whose too inconceivably

deeply ensepultured existence may
know no light brighter than a note which drops
down from the surface where it may not say
a word of where it came from, but still chops
its message up, as though to mention day
were to prevent it, or to be what stops
my painful gills, until this ocean bed
receive and rack me with its hating dead.

Eight of two threes and then a final two,
leaf three on three until the last pair shuts
these three parts up alive & passible as who
numbers his flesh according to the cuts
which self-inflict its thinking. So that you
count from set figures these unending gluts :
one in three faces, two wills and two natures
whose emanations are the living creatures.

Then if I should expire inside this box
I live in inks until the grain's deposit
settle ubiquitously and unlocks
in each who needs it what they need not posit
but just know suddenly, as life knows knocks
without a theory, since the flesh just was it :
now from mere numbers may these winter flowers
burst in the middle of the night's white hours!

Or each compresses serifs to a knot
of lost calligraphies, whose tender swashes
cleave to each other in the tightest dot
waiting disravelments : so this black washes
the stone heart brighter from its close-knit blot
when strokes uncramp into a line which quashes
with one quick flash immoveable despair,
restores the healthy to true disrepair.

I read salvation from the tea leaves : each
begins to move beneath my patient look.
Each knows a letter or may just then reach
its outline as a number : then this book
grows with each patterning or each sweet pleach
figure on figure makes, until I brook
the last stuck sump of my recalcitrance
where even I take up my bed and dance,

so I must forecast from the special taste
which lines my mouth in this persisting room.
A certain savour of repulsive waste
implies that from this intranspicuous gloom
I must surge up into the light, replaced
in very daylight, as the flightless zoom
in thought's quick minute where I point to rescue
bliss to the letter with a little fescue.

I think of walking in the afternoon
just at that hour of winter when the west
is lit at its low edge; the pale flat moon
hides in the east, and all the upper rest
of the large sky is dark with cloud where soon
that dark will thicken, yet retain, suppressed,
some corrugations and some folds of light
lined in its grey mass, till the coming night

intensify behind those sheets its deeper
shades of true lightlessness : yet in idea
for now I walk towards a bright or steeper
far precipice of setting, where the sheer
edge of continued daylight keeps each sleeper
awake on earth : the hour of mingled fear
and deep tranquillity, where recollection
recovers every feeling from dejection

into this slow walk on a high bank raised
just at the west edge of the brimming drain
where in cold grass and mud my feet are phrased
in even paces, like the patient strain
of measured prose in whose returns I praised
each several runnel, each release of rain
to ditch, fen, pond, marsh, river, bog and level
as though each water were the edge you bevel

in all these intersecting nets of wet
lines & rough stanzas : and the late dim sun
bursts suddenly afire, when it is let
out of the cloud bank, and my walk may come
through to where majesty of how it set
breaks on the dun flats and lights up this one
perfectly insignificant procession
five miles along the line of dispossession

where ocean was defeated, and those isles
are changed to hills which dominate the low
fields and the meadows, while the straightest aisles
bisect each part of them. I still may know,
here in this room, those former outdoor trials
of spirit's nerve against the dirt I go
five miles in thought through every night at three
just when the darkness have collected me

into impossibility of leisure.
There is no surface where my mind can sleep :
no refuge from reflection; no set measure.
O in the middle of the night I keep
reverting to the thought of your displeasure.
My high anxieties drop down the steep
gulf of my fixed heart where I quail and tremble
remixed in panics I may not dissemble.

Farewell, lost summers of the belle époque!
Your undeluded clarity let streams
of purest crystal run along and mock
the heavy seriousness of my dark themes.
One rustic maiden in a pretty smock
might be that goddess whose inclined brow deems
a long procession of these fears or terrors
the least indelible of simple errors,

and with a slight laugh or a cheerful word
might just abolish them, and let dissolve
each cloudy thought into a tune she heard
sung on the barricades, whose shared resolve
knows with one fleet step of its mind absurd
these prayers, hymns; as I should solve
all superstition with the fairest line
cut as hellenic or a serpentine

flex of the pen, to leave the whitest flank
set on the page in beauty. So that reason
make with one curve the beautifullest blank
passage of limb, and the delighted season
bring its etched garlands where the state may thank
the genial correctors of unreason :
where nymphs repel with sceptical advances
dark mantras, incantations, ghasts and trances.

The young fate wishes to delete the mass
of stormy gloom which gathers in the sky :
her cloudless mind repudiates the class
of pseudo-concepts. In a mirror I
can see no trace of her; imagined grass
lets her disport herself amongst the high
group of true intellects, whose real interiors
are immaterially the superiors

of flesh-kept petals, kneaded clays and pelt.
Their possibilities reserve a mode
of free reflections, whose preferred unfelt
currents of argument need no abode
more real and earthly than the print which spelt
a silent logic silently bestowed
on each mind whose precise interpretation
requires no human noise nor intonation.

Farewell the thought field of the cloth of gold
whose entertainments may not be depicted :
the muted vowel whose number is not told
retires expressively from this inflicted
count of cut gems, the purely mental fold
known where each verbal item is restricted.
Art in print's cortex is what still subtracts,
from austere lineation, mere flat facts.

I may not know the graveyard by the sea.
Its monuments, its quaterfolds, its tens,
convoked by numbers alien to me
persist impassively. Each sum extends
the logic of its thought phonology
into an order which my mind half sends
to stellar distance, airless purity,
as what may mortify that which in me

should never peep at its aristocratic
manage and sweep, nor know its proper lightness,
but thump back heavily some theocratic
stump of stress-timing to drown out that rightness,
sink verse arithmetic in automatic
beats, steps and marches, so that floated brightness
may always inaccessibly retreat
before that tread of too-emphatic feet.

I never can be French; syllabic hues
of word's transparency disperse in white
just where the next thought on the space I choose
inks up its dances on excess of bright
unpaginated terraces : refuse
each clumsy figure & each wilful flight.
They know instead the long serenity
of merely gazing on the sunlit sea.

The more appearances, the more the real
may without effort be at once detained
into what knows it does not need to peel
that surface which is what must be retained
in its phenomenality : I feel
these and just these thoughts when I am restrained
from populating their precise perceptions
with personations and prepared deceptions.

I must repeat those blows which I expected
even before a single one arrives :
so scorn sticks closely to my resurrected
bone of set metre, whose strong rhythm thrives
on any affect given to reflected
wrong stripes of feeling when the beat just drives
the single spool of lines still too protected
in just that mockery which its dejected

life would still shelter in. It won't come out.
The unconditional returns to pain
as thought to prophylactics, nurses doubt,
since it would parenthetically stain
the very exit shut, and be about
nothing at all sooner than know again
this answerable face of recognition
or speaking twin of print's devolved cognition.

It was my chrysalis : I can escape
now from the very feeling that a line
must mean I wear a gag or seal with tape
prose mouth or verse mouth when the words are mine
only so far as yours too. No more drape
the necklace with dead nightingales! Refine
with purer sense each word; I may walk free
from nugatory beauties, and may see

the split line on the ironstone alone
for its own moving contour : I may go
in thought through all the villages of stone
without a single symbol, since I know
I do not need a theory to come home,
nor is it necessary that I show,
by some exemplary device of hurt,
I scrub the human patinas of dirt.

Then in idea every ruined brick
glows inconsolably, until these shades
fall on its surface, and the twilight's thick
slant of illuminations through the glades
dapple each damp-course like a pretty trick
of light's undying glimmer when it fades
little by little on the little cluster
of walls and buildings lit with this rich lustre.

The year's night closes, and a thought of light
grows in this jet box. Undiminished dark
is no jot brighter; the idea of sight
or memory of lime trees in the park
keep me awake now as I long for white
snow to descend again and dress their bark
in brilliant blankness where the sun reflected
warms and irradiates the resurrected

face of all nature. I remember what
has not yet been, since its imagined features
never were human; yet each several dot
could not be visible without this creature's
curve of conjecture. So from what is not
I think the not yet, while my silent teachers,
rock, hill and valley, never say a word,
content that every truth remain unheard.

Innumerable as the dead I hear
their noiseless colloquy in trees and stones :
I break the prohibition set by fear
on knowing life in the rejected bones :
I listen out now when the song comes near;
I know each detail of its thinking tones
when it addresses, hails, arrests and names me
into that shape which sings me and explains me.

The far clouds are invisible; the sky
is featureless with black, and so I gaze
on nothing's image where I may descry
inexorable longing : count the ways
into that swift reduction where all my
least nuances of sensing are what stays
impermanently in their proper bed,
the soul's contagion from the unlost dead.

Apollo grips me by the throat and chokes
the last lies out of me : so I affirm
nothing less literal than what then cloaks
song's truth in no slip but its own true turn
just when I croak, and he at once revokes
his strangulations so that I may learn
letter by letter how to call down fire
into your larynx, where I know desire.

I must change every cell : I must be born
against the little scraps where I invested
too much, deflected; my black flag be torn
into those tatters where the light protested
its solidary note, and I be shorn
of each least alibi, be tried and tested
in this quick fire, and, melted into air,
stand with those solids which are burning there.

Farewell, farewell, the life that lives together,
housed in collective hatred of the mind!
Farewell to farewells, since their ringing Never
creeps back to Egypt for a taste of blind
golden calf funtime. I instead dissever
only my own knots, so that I may find
each fear and wish as naked as the day,
known for themselves in any word I say.

Now I remember the policeman : he
stood at the exit, and his unmarked jacket
in purest black, unspoken secrecy
with pointed stare into my face, his racket
of unidentifiable unfree
chains of commandments, where my weak non placet
fell like mere error, as I tried to look
cool and determined, yet could not unhook

my terror from his stare, or fail to falter
into face-fugues. His jacket was a sheen
of matt black polymers which could not alter,
each perfectly divorced from what had been
its first real element. This counter-psalter
did down song blankly from its dark serene
hectares of flatness, where its badgeless threat
intoned monopoly of violence, met

in every inch of it, where no reflection
comes but the light sucked down into his coat.
The dire absorbent grave of recollection
eats it down dead inside the open throat.
I flinch in opposites of intellection,
found all too human at law's lawless note,
state's nameless face who sees my each least part,
then penetrates insensibly my heart.

It is the corpse of polity which stirs
with unacknowledged malice in his features :
a disidealized disdain inters
all recollection of the living creatures :
no reason need be given : he prefers
not to say who he is, and that must reach us
as more than we need know, where who protested
already is internally arrested.

A hundred million cameras watch each other,
capturing data just in case the gifts
should slip past money, and the hated mother
fail to be audited : each instant lifts
cash to the pyramid. Death kiss death's other
here in the teller, where the cash-suck sifts
all trust and love to drop into the bin,
death's death's-head sugar to be welcomed in.

The world shrinks to an analytic judgement.
Its self-identity is sealed asleep
into itself : each quality is bludgeoned
into some quantity, nor may it keep
one faint aroma of its grace, one grudging
grasp of its own breath, but is locked down deep
into automatisms of the free
choice which predestinates each part of me.

A single thought, a single horde of locusts
stripping each cell of meaning from the earth :
earth's individual virus, earth's known focus
gripping to death each felt return of mirth :
zero, denominating hocus-pocus
all corporeal exit from wealth's dearth :
one blank, one itch, one number, one fat sum,
one fixed apostasy till kingdom come.

It hunts down angels in the very nook
it first has firebombed : it must twice abolish
what it has murdered, so the slightest look
need never greet it from the thrice demolished
shepherd republic, and its one dumb book
print them extinct, and then politely polish
off each squealed remnant of collective song.
Wo ich war, soll es werden, and the throng

of real experiences must be stashed
under the fascia. Yet this can not be :
I can know, at the moment I am lashed
to masts of capital, that, inside me,
there is what feels, whenever it is smashed,
particulars of smashing. To the sea
my thoughts like ash fly out, and at that ocean
each reconvenes to life its thrice-burnt notion.

There at the brink I hear the sounding wave
crash and recover like a failing heart :
I watch each crest collapse into its grave
as though the whole of it in every part
were that wet body which alone could save
life to its single necessary art
of maritime expectancies, the far
discernible horizon and one star.

Its sole tumultuous recursion beats
in blind assaults upon a patient shore.
Its shoal of foam converges, breaks and eats
each stone a little with its steady roar.
Its grey mass gathers all withdrawn defeats
into advances, and the flowers it bore
rest on the surface of the sea-wracked strand.
In utter weakness they adorn that sand

while as I stand in thought and gaze into
the western limit, I again renew
my inner littoral; I am like who
has his own coasts, his inlets of a spirit
cut in the helix which he must inherit
by this and just this history. Bright bar
of lit air in the west! and brighter star,
shine temporarily, until where you

look out now, in my mind, the darkness covers
each little thought, and I shall sleep at last.
I saw the tracks of angels in the waves.
Fear held me rigid when the spirit-lovers
flew to my side & had my breast gripped fast
into their radiances, and they cast
each cowering atom of me into speech,
each hand and foot into its proper reach.

Shew my dark speech upon the harp or bring
its silent substance to the touch : declare
in shadowed notes my first of love, and ring
on each slow chime that thirst, above which there
brood spirit-figures, since to each mute thing
the magic circle of her voice and hair
sings it transfigured, and its mesh wakes freshened,
resuscitated, risen, flesh-impressioned.

That neck which bristles at a note or air
capturing perfectly the best flown thought
can lose its nerve, can stupefy, can tear
the link of noticing, and then what ought
to lift the skin to razors, just sits there
like the dumb object-body's armour, fort
braving experience to the very coffin,
sealed in that fuselage which it took off in.

The spiritual organs vegetate
into their own legitimations, hooked
each to a total of the packs it ate :
so vision blinded by the box which looked
in proxy colours logs the time & date
on every image, as a mouth might cook
each bite itself, an ear, a nape should feel
only those symbols which it might unpeel

as information. When the unzipped ticket
prints head first from the nose, and masks its odours
deep in the tax gap, then do not just lick it :
self-sabotage the portals, quick decoders,
fill it with that sand into which you stick it.
May these devices be the sweet imploders
releasing quiddities to every palate,
heft to the hammer and the heavy mallet!

I stand and stare into this eastern night.
Across the sleepless city I can see
land-constellations of the points of light
sketch where the vallies or the hills might be,
obliterated; motorways, whose right
lines cut sublime arcs through the dark dim sea
of field and hill and wood, where quiet shade
retreats obscurely from the bright things made.

It is as grand and as sublime as hell;
the fiery pathways of incessant cars
stream with their lit directions & each shell
of rubber, steel and plastic, bears its stars
in rapid channels where the tarmacs fell
down from the ridges. Spies and commissars
mingle in each flow, where all private travel
sticks in a public thread from which unravel

these individual segments. This immense
topography of routes unfolds in neon
right to the far edge where the failing sense
founders & fails, where the most distant peon
walks there invisibly, too hidden in the dense
dark at the roadside. As austere as Creon,
the massive edifice denies a grave
to each loved relative : the metal wave

bears them away to where they are cremated.
There is no graveyard at the city's edge.
Smoke just ascends, so that each dead belated
instance disperses, while the hurting wedge
fixes its grille to grin in an unstated
grimace of malice, whose menace & whose pledge
is second nature in the solar plexus,
live burial of each soul in the nexus.

The mechanisms of this Phlegethon
hurtle towards their burning mouth : they come
as calmly and as deafeningly on
as ever incandescent car or dumb
containers hauled up to the top, then gone
over the lip into some blank or some
still unseen territory, where they drive
almost as though they really were alive.

The quiet map of night : it spreads and gathers
dot by lit dot until the flock of shining
adorns each rise and fall. The dark land gathers
beneath those gems, as though this fire's refining
sent it to carbons. So its dim sweep gathers
into this pleat, these ridges, realigning
each human setting in huge curves of rock,
while still behind me clicks the ticking clock.

That noise of waters which I cannot hear
resounds beneath the traffic : its unsleeping
torrents of men and fuel make the sheer
facts of this basin. I stand here unweeping
while the deleted feeling crashes near
by wave and wave, until estranged work steeping
each precinct of the city in its cash
engulfs & buries it in tar and ash.

A tune still pipes up in my toneless brain;
however many sectors of it are
sworn to oblivion, still this hardy strain
crops up again unbidden, since there are
in this bone box those cheek-twists, that refrain,
which like the cockle in the wheat just are
near ineradicable, since they pop
up in my head the more I try to stop

their vents of hearing. So I find when I
am halfway from the window to the bed,
from bed to window, and the blackened sky
calls from its centre, or a sudden dread
grips me when I am at the sink. I try
just not to listen to what's in my head
where at an instant very hell may shine
incorporated in a single line.

Then though the case of eyes looks straight ahead
the inward organ is detained at home :
I stare straight forward, as though vision sped
right to the target, to its final Rome,
yet all the colours ring around my head
into polyphony whose present dome
is the skull's soundless backboard, which I beat
with speech which shades into the sung or sweet

score of poured cogitations, whose profuse
thoughts and surmises scatter on the air,
perfectly fugitive. No earthly use
may be assigned to them; their dark or fair
self-involutions issue in a loose
shower of phonemes, and I once more stare
here by the window, fixed in vacant gazing
out to those wounded hills and all their blazing

stripes of reiterated light. They flay
the still receiving earth whose silent frame
in mute anticipation of the day
awaits inaudibly. Your secret name
is hidden in the hollow : what you say,
dispersed forever, cannot be the same,
but floats and trembles in the heavy air
until it disappear. You still stay there,

and this whole map of land becomes your face.
Each incline, outcrop, precipice, descent
refuses blank neutrality, mere space :
each owns the pressure which it was and meant
as nature were already thick with grace
sown in the fresh field where I pitch my tent
and walking through the undeluded earth
like the warm pattern of eluded dearth.

I can see none of this, but where I see
the phosphorescent strips of traffic lanes
punish and hold it, there revert to me
resisting negatives, as though earth's pains
were each thus itemized, and each should be
real as a figure for the life that wanes
where the choked public shrivel into cash
or state unwithering commend to ash

the whole junked culture. Let it burn in me :
let its demise inform each phrase and line,
bad immolation of the truth set free
these bitter cinders, which refuse to shine
more than this ink upon the page may be
an undead letter. For no thought is mine :
each still comes to me from the dead whose style
murmurs indelibly despite all vile

drugs of forgetting. I can plan a walk
straight up the dual carriageway : the east
holds scattered friends, whose unforgotten talk
sounds in my head now from the very least
of exile clusters. So I wish to walk
five hundred miles into the shrouded east :
in each incinerated town a brother,
in each wrecked house a father and a mother.

Vox sine verbo, how you strive to let
word's meaning to its uttered parturition!
All birthpangs wrack the paralanguage set
in vocalises of mere inanition
that the thought logos stop the vox pop yet
retain each contour of just this audition
into this wilderness where I just cry
one hundred years too late, until I die.

The rent veil of the temple knows a broke
gold standard when it hears one : so there quiver
in live refusals of the numbered yoke
distant transactions of the banks which shiver
into a million. Cinnamon and smoke
get up their noses, so the corporate giver
requires some looser garment, has me speak
in disarticulated prose or weak

lines where a breeze come through may let me know
the taste of weather, and allow my chant
soon to fall silent. It is time to go;
I would stay here forever, but I can't
eat air indefinitely; even so,
I cannot make my feet move, like what shan't
shift one inch when necessity speaks plain,
as I-can't-hear-you were its deaf refrain.

I need not wear that tie which is embedded
deep in my throat : invisible command
grips at the larynx softly while my shredded
Systemprogramm deletes itself. My hand
thinks all its actions are intended – threaded
back to the head – but down into the sand
go signals, gestures, menaces and squeaks,
each still foresuffered in the mud which speaks.

What he called outward ceremony is
my sole left inner aperture : without
this certain precinct on the map there is
only the flux of signals, whose sweet doubt
feeds blind addiction as though what there is
were all just nothing, and the one way out
a fairy story whose unlikely end
insists on an imaginary friend.

Hit me with that again! Imagination
dreams nothing up but the forgotten real.
The very substance of this single nation
depends upon capacity to feel
the real unseen, whose cruel evacuation
is then the alibi for how we steal
their labour from our slaves : the eye won't see
what heart don't grieve for, so if I won't be

here at all really, but just represented,
I may do anything I like to them.
Bad city, how you need that still resented
sum of all good, to whose abolished hem
you cling with scholia which disinvented
true, good and beautiful, from just which stem
even your flowers of prevented malice
blossom & flourish in non-love's blank palace.

I am that city in my secret heart.
I reprehend it, but each globe of blood
runs through that centre my continued art
of self-evasions. Antiphons are dud
when what they answer to can own no part
not pre-responsoried : so my first mud
clothes & contaminates whatever skin
I use to put this self-transcendence in.

Therefore it is essential that I know
one individual building where that pulse
may be suspended, and those proteins go
still with a different rhythm : a repulse
to nature's nature severs there the flow
with all fixed strictures which must still revulse
that little bit of bone which takes itself
for the flat absolute. There on the shelf

a little statue stands impassively.
It may not suffer, since its metal knows
no sentience whatever; it is free
from all intelligence; its riven pose
holds the same thin arm out upon the tree
in tiny replication of that rose
known in the real cross of unyielding stuff
digested grain by grain. It's not enough

to eat the bread or drink the bloody wine :
this meal of detail is the hourly feast
into whose each least desecration shine
all still miscopied doctrines. In the east
it is as though the sun forgot to shine
since utter darkness rules out the deceased
edge where the light is meant to break and bring
illuminations and the twice born king.

I am exhausted, yet I may not rest.
I scan black heaven, yet no single comet
flares on its flat expanse : I fail this test,
unable to do more than bring back from it
baffled aridity. Just do your best :
this means, just give up, write the symbolled sonnet
interinextricably wired with this
deputed syntax, theory's lipless kiss.

Father, you dwindle in the gapless night.
I may no longer hear your voice : I see
your face before me, but my failing sight
blurs at the edges, and I cannot be
brought to the remnant of your chosen light
but lose you steadily, until for me
at last no trace or record will remain.
You will recede, and your abolished train

leave no unearthly glimmer in the sky
not super-allocated into that
theory of immanence whose blinded eye
sees itself only. Soul's last Ararat,
chink in the prism of the world where I
cut open dry land, spirit's single slat,
numbers whose substance is a wordless question,
be now my medium of sung suggestion!

Sustain in me, continually beaten,
reviled interrogations of the whole :
make of those substances which I have eaten
their own true taste, and let the common bowl
deny, derided, what privations sweeten.
Extend instead this universal dole,
reverse each cage into its first light cloak,
each stern decree into a kindly joke.

So I address you in the second person :
the first must decrease, and the third draws off
into the middle distance. When I worsen,
restrain, revive, restore me : raze, rub off
those oxidations, wrong's well-wrought unperson
stuck in my throat as if it would choke off
your word which wants to get into the air
and dance like fury. Burn, blow, break and tear

the thin film over me, until I know
each instant's secret absolute, each thing
named into paradise, as though to go
just with my finger on a map would sing
the land's trapped anthems, and each place could show
its own word as the image of a king
whose imminent arrival were the last
future discovered in the shining past.

The new priest faces inwards, as though he
were the convenor of our hopes and fears :
the old one stares east, since, with this look, we
are constituted as a person; hears,
in the least rustle of the night, unfree
perambulations of the planets. Years
roll away quickly from this single altar,
fixed by a set gaze which may never falter.

Emperor penguins in the bitter winter
know the right method not to freeze to death :
each is pushed outward from the group's warm centre
to take a turn at suffering where breath
solidifies incessantly; cold's splinter
lacerates each. By one and one as death
pushes me further to the tribe's outside
I stare all night into the dark divide

just as my father stared before me, since
next up for nothingness, air's vacant edge.
At that fixed limit all the brilliant tints
drain from life's repertoire; at this met ledge
I throw away the talismans and hints
which brought me to it; here at last no hedge
may save bets backwards, but the very stones
implode in payment of their own first loans.

I cannot see you in that element.
The more you vanish into intermittence,
the more my speech, my gestures, all sound sent
straight from your face, as though direct transmittance
held me implacably to what you meant,
more like you every day, the live remittance
of your continuous and watchful care.
You yourself are me now you are not there.

So when I look into the east where you
are now no longer to be found, I know
right at my westward stand the others, who
have not arrived yet at their time to go.
I block their vision now; when I am through,
they shall see clearly, as the fallen snow
melts to reveal each part of grass and earth
patiently waiting for its painful birth.

Buds of the spirit break up from my skin
rooted inextirpably to this room :
so my burst surface knows the state I'm in,
law's undirempted ethics of the tomb;
the soul is unprivated, since its kin
sing from inside it, where its father's womb
contracts with love, racked, swollen, lifted, torn
until this recollected thought be born.

That first flung crying is the real new note
of what it must be like to breathe the air.
The helpless infant feels its sudden throat
invaded, filled, and aided : each lung there
opens with noises which may not denote,
but whose sung substance is appeal for care,
first hymn, first prayer, which our livings-on
attempt to extirpate its whole life long.

It is the purest tone of kindred feeling,
the one intolerable sound on earth;
its call for succour overtops the reeling
of all alarms, because it sings down dearth
when prae-existently its grammar pealing
from right inside the hid mind comes to birth :
first incantation whose sweet tones foreknow
each feat of accidence it may forego.

Each tense and case lies folded in the mind.
At just this instant of the first loud cry
each is awoken into human kind
just as that tender speech with which I fly
to soothe and mother, cradle, rock and find
more or less anything to pacify
the same loud wawling in my buried chest
and seal the banished heart up in the breast.

A raging lion calls out in the head.
The new-born antiphon of thought to thought
sounds like a bell, because a tongue's tone shed
from the inexpert mouth resounds in taut
foundation of whatever can be said
or exposition of the still unbought
dyad of love and rage, the church and state
cleaving together when believed too late.

It is not nature when you live : high panic
calls all the dryads to their slots, but you
move in repose, so that the claimed organic
life of tradition is instead run through
with graceful interruptions, inorganic
cuts and corrections where the page shows through
& all that serious writing is borne up
on intonations to its loving cup.

The tree with vocatives in all its branches
works with its knowledge through the sons of Eve :
you send appeals whose sap no quick fire stanches;
steel of imperatives I must believe
opens my side too, where it stops and blanches
blood's wish for blood. Sustain me, undeceive
each dumb slump back into the habit coat
by recapitulating just that note.

I have no mystery but what I am
commanded to become : this métier
hems in the middle, as a block or dam
puts up restrictions, and the shut flood may
irradiate rejoicing in the lamb
since in each obstacle you are the way
wished & demanded in the tongue's quick thicket,
fished out, remanded at the lung's thick picket.

Dioxins shaped into melodious air
speak with sweet reason when they will disperse
into those echoes; who receives them there
is quite uncertain, and their deaf reverse
decodes a thought part from its unsung pair
as prose makes up the very line of verse.
So into disenchantments I must tread
these footsteps of the undeluded head.

Wax on the pages from the unclean hand
makes the pen tremble; I must slip or swerve
where ink slides sideways from the thought I planned
into its own less imbecilic curve
which drowns the text out with a marching band
of swoops and serifs, as though you deserve
that sortilege of adorations thrown
from ink's black happenstance to purest tone.

These are the apaugasmata : these beams
of white noise find out the supposed absconded
father of lights, and at their dark extremes
each gives out kindly into this unbonded
wildness of night, whose uncorrected dreams
work at the true word where his love responded.
So the day's residues in happy lapses
slip into clarity through blank collapses.

Today in flesh among the beasts, but then
torn amidst thieves, hung up to desiccate.
Today a little chit, but when those men
nail him up good, the sacrifice of hate.
Today he cries until that instant when
crosses constrain him to a spoken fate
and sussurations must be put away
with all the tongue's toys till another day.

X marks the pattern of my forward march.
Each step I plant upon receding ground
declares strong progress, yet the backward arch
of all unconscious losses must resound
under my soles. I suck on fat and starch,
eating feet forwards, until I am found
rigid as stone heads, and my fixed expression
gurns for posterity stone's own confession.

Each of these words is heard in Ascalon.
Although I swallow them, recording sprites
get them off pat, so that the least thing gone
is held indelibly, until pain's rights
are abrogated, and those lights which shone
on infant wordlessness are snuffed in spite's
perfected chronicle of how I failed,
as waves remembered each wrong ship which sailed.

I don this ephod, and the poison shirt
sticks to my skin revivingly : it preys
only on that strength which would do strong hurt
to all those under it. Its false amaze
reverses on that officer whose pert
name, rank and number meet my equal gaze,
determination to return his stare
supported by no power but thin air.

Pitch your pavilion in my breast : let me
construct no fictive image of you there,
but let the fact of you arise in me
as just that army which can live on air
& make no mock, refuse to take a fee,
its spirituous edifice declare
rapacious hosts of uncommanded love
scorching all earths as they retire above.

The last black antiphon is sung apart :
the singers are not visible, reserved
to an adjoining aisle; my heart
is struck down on the spot, and its deserved
account of breakage rendered by that dart
lopping all habits from the skin they curved
back to its bad face when the wind blew wrong,
the needless grimace I wear all night long.

He longs to be depleted : since I drink,
just this replenishes his depthless fountain.
I draw each drop down into what I think,
drain thought's drowned rivers from the one left mountain.
I see more instantly with each hot blink,
learn the grand galop as refined dismounting,
lose out the best until my eyes fur up
enough to get these blocked lips to the cup.

Full inexhaustibly of truth and grace,
but grace came first, since truth's true incandescence
could not be born unless some kinder face
were in appearance essence of its essence;
this & just this set order of the phrase
locates eternity in evanescence :
I blush, quail, tremble and avert my eyes
willing and willing that the sun not rise.

Day, break from breaking : I am buried sweet
right in the lap of darkness, where I know
delights so secret that the very teat
of strong narcotics, or the lightless glow
shed by desire sewn back into the pleat
of its own self-reflections may not go
above it, nor the rush of pretty fires
burn so deliciously in private pyres.

I am embellished on the lip of day,
a figure which revokes it and refuses
each little opening, since its own closed way
is to furl up now from what still accuses
into a single point, whose pleasure may
never be found out. I am what recuses
itself back down forever into dark,
night's brightest blindness, wrong's remaindered ark.

I cannot know what comes or hopes to wake me.
Each little tap upon my skull's thick wall
sounds faint and distant, as it could not make me
even perceive it, since I give my all
to those same obduracies which may slake me.
Eject me, strip, describe me, still I fall
into indelible self-sentience,
out of the world into the sense of sense.

Here at the furthest watch of night I think
imagined candles burning at the far
end of my thoughts, as though their winters' brink
were concentrated there, or one faint star
shone thru this one slit & upon that drink
trembled the reflex like a sign there are
unthought-of spirits in the sky's black blank
from which assembly one escaped beam sank

here to this cup, whose surface is disturbed.
A breath curls lightly on the fluid top
as though a four-inch lake were thus perturbed,
stood in my hand, from which I might let drop
its shaking waters. Stellar rays inferred
just at the lip here may blink up or pop
finer than gems, whose stony play of light
cannot be noticed in this perfect night.

A human solstice in work's global ocean,
one day's renunciation of the glut;
a single fault inside the gapless notion,
one opening achieved by what is shut;
a flexing line through pixelized commotion,
soul's folded secret which may not abut
exchanges, prices, tokens, brands or stamps,
dark ground of seeing to the brightest lamps.

Inside the thickest darkness comes a sound
whose scintillations may not be dispelled
since all its flickerings are stuck and bound
down to the root which flung them upwards, held
in sallies and reveilles which resound
from brick to brick until they seem to meld
with blocks and buttresses, stone's standing joy,
radiant persistence or celestial toy.

Electric filaments preserve a thread
burning at will, as though the daylight were
just mine to summon, and my stubborn head
might be switched on whenever I prefer
to think up wizards. Every skin I shed
sits by my side, since I may not confer
parthenogenesis on this hot button,
lamb of revival in its undressed mutton.

I must die, so life's undiminished question
is that first substance of essential wonder
which with the power of its lit suggestion
illuminates the very sound of thunder,
salts the sweet meat down to my slow digestion,
seals up the wrong law which would merely sunder
object from object, as the world's dry goods
lay on a table with its oughts and shoulds.

It is impossible for me to turn
from that memento mori which I find
almost gives life itself, since I must learn
each possibility of cruel or kind
action struck through for me : consume, then, burn
in every colour of the sun your mind
through to its final epitaph of ash,
its charred sum total, carbonized to cash.

Or some last part of me were still curated
down in a field with a laconic stone
as though my patient skeleton awaited
a call from Jesus, when my sleeping bone
should with a hop and skip from its belated
six feet of earth jump up, and this alone
keep the deep marrow of my life intact,
hell's weeping harrow in the silent fact.

The dead must fight then for their proper ditches,
since the whole surface of the written earth
is thick with signs whose signifying itches
glitter obliterating bone's first birth
here from the consecrated mud, whose niches
have all been allocated. Then let mirth
refute earth's toxic maximum : stand up
dead centre, life's peripheries, bright cup!

My brain would rather almost anything
than bear the labour of the concept : I
know, in these intermezzi, that torqued ring
to keep each shape of feeling from the sky
or be that labyrinth in which each thing
thinks it may be transmuted, or defy
thought's ceaseless work which leaves it only ready
to topple instantly from its unsteady

place on the shelf, where these two idol-brothers
shove at each other. Work on the idea
cannot but be resumed; it thus recovers,
into its painful inches, real fear,
subtending all those concepts whose locked others
shade them insensibly beneath the sheer
imageless logic of that single name
which might unlock, from this self-sealing game

one act of reference, one rough edge of rock.
My hand runs lightly on the pebbledash
here at the sill, as I still feel the shock
of freezing air across the half-healed gash
in my left arm; from this pain I now dock
each instant one more property, then stash
deleted qualia where you can't find them.
I take the living creatures and I bind them

far below sentience. Now they are quiet.
I cannot now hear anything at all.
A call still silenced by the lungs which cry it,
a counter-Eden, just unfit to fall;
a death inaudible to those who die it,
tongue turned to rubber in the empty mall :
these are the instances which sing – 'it's actual',
then tell me 'everything is satisfactual'.

O grex immolatorum tener, you
are still, embodied far beyond the night :
144,000 who
refuse to be commanded. At first light
you are the firstling buds, who will come through
ready to be destroyed by frost, whose bite
kills all the songbirds, each of whom I see
fall to the ground, without a word from me.

Their absent song to the abandoned earth
keens indiscernibly : its vacant miles
know nothing so determined as a curse,
but strive for disenchantment which resiles
from each deep freshness, and at last breaks verse
to those smashed instances whose violent trials
grab for some purchase where the thought gives out,
as faith lives only where there is strong doubt.

When erased skylarks from the massive field
leap at a bounce to bound into the air
their contribution to the total yield
is still foreseen as negative, so there
they might implode, before their far-sung shield
could ever be extended to repair
deaf-headed repertoire of slaves' thick wax
ear-wedged aggrandizingly to the max

& the hot tractor with its blithe combustion
cannot be fixed, but must sit still & rust.
We suck the money out with no compunction :
there is no fallow, and the dead soil must
work for a living if it wants to function
until each particle is done to dust
and total silence of the mind is found
before each fact in the repeated ground.

I am recorded as a seed that dies.
Spermatic logos, know your last reversion :
shoots, shrink back down now from the chequered skies
until that foliage, whose bright inversion
shades the lake's surface, lose to funded lies
its shape and nature, as reverse immersion
could unbaptize whoever wished to die
still undeluded, still unwashed, still dry.

I am to figure as a tic or virus
proliferation of the sung ideal.
Each of the sparks with which a flint can fire us
is to be doused, as though this were the real :
the suicidal leaf which can require us
to turn one inch the universal wheel
and know prodigious self-extermination
as the top dollar of self-preservation.

It is inevitable that the free
movement of capital prevail by force :
it has no action, so its life in me
is only what evades, is what of course
I just hand over, as the fatal tree
blooms in my throat now, and the silent source
in strong self-exculpations bubbles up,
a swift prevention between lip and cup.

Face to the pillow I would stop my head
back down to recollection, since the new
awakes in perfect abstractness, the shed
marginal gains which gather up these few
gasps of past breathings whose impelled tunes sped
in the fixed preset : so what I must do
is laid out for me like the anti-meal
I must eat up now, just as I must feel

hot innovations of his master's voice.
Products assemble in the warehouse : I
inventorize them, but the only choice
is not to choose, since each one's helpless eye
is burnt and branded, as it must rejoice
to speak its price to the indifferent sky
year in year out upon the shelf, and sit
utterly lonely till I come for it.

The household gods are stacked up in the shop.
Their folded powers are a name-tagged token :
they ping and giggle, but they may not stop
these blip-flipped vocables, nor be awoken
until bleach saturate the cloth or mop
I wipe the floor with when a flask is broken
to clean each inch down to its former glisten
and cash ring back wherever I might listen.

They are the prayer-wheels of immanence.
Their superstitious clangs and incantations
garland the street through windows in defence
against the supernatural : their stations
stand behind glass now, whence they beg expense
to fend off glory, whose wrong depredations
it is the duty of each citizen
to mask back blankly to its bog or fen.

Night's bitter crystal is the wrong revenge
for these poor idols, who may not be blamed
for what we did with them, nor their glass henge
shattered except each shatterer, defamed,
broken by breaking, as I would avenge,
by smashing something up, just that which framed
my own limbs capable to smash, or took
hurt's hurt-filled violence for a sacred book.

I gaze all night at where the bright reflections
play in the double sheet, as though this pane
were a compendium of true corrections
to the bad wish to break it. Since again
night's chosen spectrum of unfixed inflexions
skitters across the glass, I must remain
fixed to the spot before its shielded glitter
compelled to know that there is no screen fitter.

A glass of water on this arid desk.
As dawn (perhaps) approaches, and you must
depart, I tense my shoulders for a test,
a sign, a signal, as the very dust
should at a drop of rain awake confessed
in immemorial fragrances which just
refuse to let me lie down now and sleep,
retained all night into the watchful deep.

Down in the dark bed of that final ocean
no sunlight ever penetrates the wave.
There at the bottom of the sea no motion
sways the lost bones, nor can one atom crave
one new disturbance, nor one new commotion,
since at the blank foot of the empty stave
the same drowned mark prescribes eternal rest
just as least molluscs do their senseless best.

Impassibility perfects its art
in just those last sands which the long marine
current remakes in every little part,
their underwater ranges where unseen
gulfs and sharp precipices tear apart
the coldest waters, and each dark ravine
abides in silent burial unknown
as thoughts are hidden in the noiseless stone.

The light can never find me there : I sink
just in imagination to that floor
where the flood covers me, and what I think
is visibly submerged, so that when your
treble appeals with their re-echoed ink
came inundated to the tide-crushed door
of my perceptions, they in vain must cleanse
my thoughts & feelings with their song-filled pens.

Profane as Christian radio, flat chatter
renders each detail gratefully to Caesar.
There is no church where what is thought mere matter
becomes a tactic, an indifferent pleaser :
the shrunk soul leaner, but their mass grows fatter
when each plump sermon kicks off with a teaser.
I am distributed discursively
as though print's lip-work were the stuff of me.

I am abashed : I cannot but disperse
at each new moment into true occasion.
It is as though the first disgardening curse
were to distribute me as conversation :
I am replanted only in that verse
which reconvenes me from my dissipation
just in so far as I at once am sundered
into those ancestors whose strong voice wondered

inside me every time I should obscure
astonishment with the default type-token.
Their silent action is a strong and pure
reconvocation of the needful broken
hymnal of prose, and the delicious lure
is shown for abstract : so I am awoken
into that really unimagined real
whose quiddities are the revealed ideal.

I dread twelfth-night when all the lights come down
just since the domination of unreal
clock-life resumes its effort at a frown
and mathematicizes to ideal
ticks and tocked lockets, all's steel-sealed renown.
Now, accurate enthusiasm, feel
to the least point and tittle each false dot,
philologize upon one needful jot!

The duties of each hour instruct me how
I may find stations in the pathless waste.
Faith has no colour; as I peer out now
into that air I cannot see or taste
I feel no wave pass underneath no prow
but meet again that blessedness misplaced
far east or heavenwards in each checked docket
which I must verify, without a rocket.

It is impossible to just inspect
the medium where the inspector lives :
he may not handle it, still less correct
its proper contour by a rule he gives;
he must look through it, must just disconnect
from his own theory, as, when one forgives,
it is much more than just a credit note,
or seals, in water, don't reflect, they float.

Locked to mere feelings, I may still escape,
provided those are perfectly forgotten.
I would fall down and kiss the robe and cape
whose works I gaze on when the unbegotten
fire of the paraclete can coolly drape
these arms and shoulders like the lightest cotton :
so I reverse this cage to its first cloak,
this zealous edict to its first true joke.

Bless, bless the Lord, you obsolescent tropes!
Leap from your shelves inside the furthest past
that mute creation may revive its hopes
of real determinacy, as, unclassed,
I brush against it with that lip which gropes
for each slain singularity, and, last,
has each speak dialect, each hum its name,
each throw some phoneme to a silent flame.

The single copies of a written book
might find out islands where some standing house
should give them refuge. I can bear to look
into the darkness, since those seas may souse
each page in salts, and your abstracted crook
preserve instructions for how best to douse
these last transmitters, pack down Cassiodorus
as exhumation-ready for that chorus.

As palaeographers betray the word
by perfect iterations, since they hack
right at the standard which it had transferred
from hand to hand, and only seal it back
pre-laminated into this unheard
sweet research cabinet, in which they track,
avid with curiosity, each letter,
(thus the bad quarto to its drunken setter)

so to one chip I trust my skin in vain :
its smart tracks me, while I help it to find
those rhythms it can never know again.
Sand is the final resting place of mind.
It never can experience one pain,
and therefore may not think : what I would bind
into its tablet is a merest zero,
whose one-nil shuttles like a headless hero.

More lectures, duck : but time is running out.
What good is it to stare at every grain
when it drops down to spell the truth of doubt?
Why must I tell each minute of the same
as though life's total were a fixed account?
Why must I settle on the same refrain,
singing and singing that I have to die?
Why all these questions, why blind life's blind why?

Life is just obsolete; the very word
strains too much for effect, and so it is
treated as rhetoric or as absurd.
In every corner of each room there is
boxed death-vocation, where the soul incurred
those mortal penalties whose payment is
the discontinuous evacuation
of all experience, soul's self-immolation.

I keep reverting to the hammerbeam :
in January, when the chastened head
must pass through ice, as though its life should seem
ordeal by blank indifference, you led
me through the marsh where I had never been;
the gone day darkened, till at last the shed
bulb of the sun upon my upturned face
fell where you saw me by some unearnt grace

gaze up into the matrix of the saints.
A war in heaven of opposing powers
thrust from the king-post trusses swoops and feints
as though each angel might repel with glowers
its wooden roof-mate, or their winged complaints
antiphonally vivisect live hours
of antique martyrs, whose excoriations
repeat themselves in violent decorations.

Each with its sideways thrust bears up the sky
as the whole panoply of holy dead
must from their first resolvedness to die
support with martyrs each surviving head
that shops, snacks, dithers, sits around, as I
visit some churches, or go back to bed,
these wooden doctors were the sole suspensions
from instant drowning, and their reprehensions

held the slack city up from every fen
they at that instant still transpierced with light.
They fall upon each others' necks, like men
winged from mere vehemence of thought : my sight
cranes and peers upwards where the twelve times ten
still cut each other, as advancing night
matches their stares into the code for bliss,
that algorithm with no surd but this

embattlement of canopies whose kings
glare back implacably : St. Stephen's lute
unpicks continuously timber strings
which when outdescanting St. Peter's flute
concert that dissonance of these made things
into their apex, music's slayed dispute
where psaltery, drum, clarion and shawm
sprout from the knife where they were flayed and born :

each instrument of martyrdom possesses
its proper timbre, and its own racked song :
just as the gridiron for us expresses
sweet melodies from torment, so the long
bud of sung pain breaks from the club which blesses
transglorified repulsions with the wrong
tune of the absolute, fear's stripped exquisite
melisma mortifying my mere visit.

I with a fish and harp must hope to rise
by one inch from the pavement : I fall down,
struck in the middle of my face and eyes
by each non-trimmer, each too wooden frown
spoken directly to me from the skies
or be myself the spoiler when a crown
adorns the pantokrator, and I ask
for yet more credit, since the undone task

lies there inside me, and each least relapse
is spread out on the floor, where now the sun
casts one last ray, one left light, where, perhaps,
I can still catch at what is to be done
and what it must begin with, as collapse
were first step back from hell, or where I shun
from simple incapacity that brink
where I had rather topple in than think.

Thoughts in the object there at once foreknew
my poor sensations : as I cricked my neck
they still impassively remained to do
work which I guessed at, where their great wings deck
my intimations with a sense that you
were catachretically fleshed as heck,
both used and mentioned in the floating roof,
so, spirit-horseshoe, to heart's wounded hoof.

There are epiphanies whose native crib
is mental warfare : the monopoly
which the state seizes over law's first sib,
what we call violence, sets its decree
right in the pitches of our voice where glib
instructions not to raise it leave me free
only to murmur with polite restraint
that I am choking : so mouth's prose must paint

its grey in grey, and with some mild expression
garnish the passage of the silent drone.
Fists long to legislate, but blank depression
wants only privacy, as I would moan
here to myself auricular confession
just at thought's whisper, and mind's ear alone
know spirit-scourges which I misdeploy
on my imaginary, heart's best boy.

I see that dashboard like a distant star.
Fear grabs the stomach, and adrenalin
puts me awake again, as though you are
immeasurably distant, and the grin
of my close enemies from one dim car,
idling outside, lit right within
this locked room where I just sit tight and wait,
wishing and wishing that it were too late.

I drop these pages like a point of light
into your all-eradicating dump.
I reconfigure them ten times a night;
I memorize them, so the coming slump
can wipe my head clean, and the remnant bright
uninked part-papers still skip up & jump
here in my voice, my palate, teeth and face
like the wrong portrait of amazing grace.

Now they have found you, and you must ignore
just that one serif where the truth is hidden;
you cannot read them, since the thought is poor,
gummed with stuck trumpets when the thrice re-chidden
idea just iterates its blinks, and your
attention dissipates again unbidden.
Lay me aside then on a hidden shelf,
smite me, rewrite me, light me up yourself.

Drop off perhaps were wake from this long course
of intercessionary sounds : belief
works its own footmarks in the stone by force
of still reiterated habit. Brief
incessantly repeated steps, my source
of non-identical elations, chief
drug, blanket, totem, badge, inch, set or measure,
lend me insensibly your viewless treasure!

The cemetery of nobilities
had better stuff down good into the ground
berserker aristos, whose special pleas
thrust up obsidian, and whose stiff sound
muffles their violence, while the cypress trees
look anywhere but where the corpse was found
bloodied by formula, and epithet
passes down hatreds from the first wound met.

I do not press back fiction at the cut
nor can concede reality is that
mesh of kenoses, where perception, shut,
sucks on a signifier. Trim your hat :
the gallery is empty, and your rut
of being but not meaning sinks as flat
dreamed-up additions to the world's mild monsters
or extra hairpiece for the monks' sunk tonsures.

Why do I speak as though I knew the world?
The cars begin to fill the road again.
By one and one their engines are uncurled
from long sleep, and their noise along the rain
is soft as blossom when it is unfurled
first from the bud, or as the tender strain
of pianissimo violas brushed
by the same hand which instantly then hushed

the shaken strings : my work must be to lose
all this false vantage, and to listen out,
here at this window, for the note I use
to reawaken from narcotic doubt
into the day. It is as though I choose
each detail which a poem is about
only so far as they are first tune-chosen,
retrieved from that mind where they first were frozen.

Just as a baby instantly commands,
from total need, the house where he is born,
so your strong lordship from the weakest bands
with purest weeping requisitions torn
strips of your cloth to bind these wounds with hands
whose action is the opposite of scorn :
place this loud infant in the parliament
that representatives confess him sent

to reconfigure with his lalling tongue
those cruel rubrics whose collected heads
stop mouths, block ears, or infiltrate the lung.
No human hearing can dispel that dread
felt by the one who listens to the flung
descant on panic which from this straw bed
brings to their knees those kings or mages who
have really no idea what to do

but cluck back comforts to the little scrap.
His voice in utter weakness regulates
the whole house round him; in his mother's lap
he from another world illuminates
what now surrounds him, as mere stuff were rapt
to this epiphany, or courts and states
knew their true substance in this helpless centre,
from power's strong arm the powerless dissenter.

The milk of human kindness is the true
milk standard of all value, but it may
not measure anything, except one who
knows for herself its numbers tell or say
divine transactions, and the hour when you
just turned up bawling, as I am the way
were just this lesson of perpetual care
expended ceaselessly, or men might dare

to see this immaterial city fill with light
the counter-city of indifferent strangers.
City of sisters, where the fearful night
is still outfaced, and its most evil dangers
are nursed & nurtured, till these vile lures quite
vanish to nothing in their canine mangers.
The city which abolishes these kindnesses
devours law's codex in its private blindnesses.

I am as calm as a redundant church.
I sit here, looking out into the dark.
Soon its expanse of black will be besmirched
with the first point of light : the dim grey park
awaits its colours; aspen, ash and birch
quiver to think it, and the sleeping lark
anticipates unconsciously one pink
shade which eludes him, as the dew's deep drink

clusters invisibly in beads or spheres
buried in grasses whose immobile tips
stretch for that single green whose verdure clears
their sleepy parts, as my reluctant lips
are brought to speech now where there still appears
no sign of light yet, since the strong night grips
all hues and tints locked down into the black
as though forever; yet they must come back

in fifteen minutes, when I shall behold
one square of colourlessness show dark blue
just at its limit, and the sky be rolled
concave again when underneath and through
its black dish I may recognize untold
deep purple parturitions then when you
are labouring to be born into each colour
as though this night were just that womb where duller

inexorable monochromes betrayed
themselves into this spectrum, and begot
life's ineradicable rainbow made
of the whole retina, whose nerve lifts hot
scarlets and oranges which are arrayed
there in the dawn which at this hour is not
apparent yet, but still nocturnal calm
covers and shades me, and my naked arm

feels the cold air freeze all its roughened skin.
I wait in joy, as though the best delight
were the anticipated mandolin
of tuneful pigments, or the feast of sight
were most delicious in conjecture : in
those little minutes when this endless night
will soon depart, yet is completely set,
impenetrably black, the jet not-yet.

It is the oceanic amulet.
I cannot get it round my neck, but must
drown in the currents of its alphabet
to be protected, as its charm might thrust,
by verbal trifles, the defences met
in groynes and sea-walls by the sea's wet crust,
and I swim coupletted, where each art matches
salvific engines with the soul's strong latches :

so at my shores the colours in the sky
begin to bleat, or at my door this key
chinks clicks and kisses in the hope that I
might soon just open, so it can bring me
its saving palindrome, or light might fly
off from the surface of the rolling sea
into my optic nerve, and find my brain
moved to admit it, as the shining train

of pinks and crimsons bleeds into the dark
purples and indigos whose black block breaks
just at its furthest edge, or as the ark
springs its first leak, so that the pilot wakes
less certain that there may not be a shark.
My repertoire of lexical mistakes,
my sung phylactery, my happy fort
starts to self-ruinate just when it ought

since now there is no colour I should ban :
viridian and all the tangerines
hem the skirt-firmament where their threads ran
in green and orange, orange-green machines
for the ascension of one better man
or eye's diversion, where its special means
are non-iconoclastible as lent
to England's birthday for its ornament

just as to Tallahassee or Pskov
or to wherever this unceasing jingle
prays all night long until it is turned off
by oriental turquoise which would mingle
unnecessary and indifferent stuff
deliciously into the till then single
blackest of black, illusory despair
which still must snuff it at the touch of air,

as though this melancholy weight of fixed
corvée of penitence might just now end,
might with a skip elude that gaze which picks
the worst from any picture, or might lend
the background to those glimmers which unfix
nude parts of canvas which at once then send
a brilliant absence in the paint to please
as foam can dazzle from the darkest seas

or double basses set off ocarinas
as no delight could be too insubstantial
to make some part of day, or celestinas
were more of essence than just circumstantial
or metre needn't spoil a line by Wieners
but just go with it, when a pen could cancel
just with a light stroke all that heaviness
which isn't needed, since, if you're depressed,

that labyrinth won't help you. Now I feel
one little current of a milder air
undress my face, this madrigal of real
shoots and tips buried underneath the square.
It is as though their flowers might unseal,
four months from now, locked fragrances from where
I had sublated them, as though their disappearance
could be reversed in a repressive clearance.

The possible Tehuantepec is held
just past the limit of my lexicon :
as the suspended tanager compelled
to wait for daylight, or the muskrat gone
into some line renounced, I am dispelled
to those epochal bracketings which shone
only in absence, since their native darkness
makes up the soul's impenetrable fastness.

I never shall attain to Florida :
I must imagine it, or hope that buds
come through the letter box one day. Those far
perplexities of palm trees, shimmered suds,
are unexpended capital : no car
excels the desert, since retentive muds
at last receive it, when its crimson spray
goes down disastered into starless day.

I cannot look into the west : this vent
opens towards the earth's immortal morning.
It is as new as what was always sent,
the luminous imperishable dawning
straight from the golden horde whose warlike tent
pitches itself here, and one side's wide awning
illuminates me in the climbing light
as I still struggle to forget the night.

Far at my back across the dark Atlantic
stretches the theory of continual freedom :
its mere idea has me almost frantic
with sharp elations, as though freedom's reason
were to abolish even the semantic
field of mortality, or reason's freedom
think me emblazoned in a red Corvette
as, if I could mix with its metal, yet

retain this sentience, shut down slow death,
I Get Around without a single breath.
Zeniths and sugars of the pink guitar!
Combust yourselves into these pining rhymes
whose *Frühlingssehnsucht* for those things which are
impossible to know, would beat their times
to incontaminable liberties! Ice tsar,
shatter your logo to its first bright dimes!

Low dips the star : the gaze drops and relapses
over the pool, where candy colours are
leaping & falling; so, where each relaxes,
I'd choose this vacancy; I'd fill the far
twists of light cloud with fancy, whose flight taxes
a summer evening, slightest line. The star,
zealous to burn, is made to slip its glimmer :
zero reflection makes the tip burn dimmer.

These sacraments of absolute consumption
require a perfect silence in the mind.
Routine excesses of profane resumption
glitter with signs before they gag and bind.
All summer from ascension to assumption,
urging my cruel flesh to the thought of kind,
I work instead to glorify true leisure :
pain's shame-razed doctrine of work-unsmirched pleasure.

Recall that summer at this frozen sill.
However I imagine colours there
I only think of them; the whole sky still
refuses to divulge them, and the air
now from each part of it begins to fill
with what drops down along my solemn stare
revisiting this window where I know
the imperturbable descent of snow.

Killed all day long, I venture out at night
just in so far as I allow my sense
to turn down inwards, as my fasting sight
feasts on that absence where I recommence
the work of looking eastward for the light.
Now all excursions drop back to their dense
layers & thickets. I am almost through;
the snow redoubles, and I think of you

buried in white upon a hillside, bent
down by your burden, by the weight of souls
accumulating from the word you meant
to set them free. The earth's unpeopled poles
keep in unyielding ice a permanent
memorial of this; the sea's deep shoals
of rays, whales, hammerheads and minor fishes
keep to themselves their fish-shaped thoughts and wishes.

What is unutterable is untrue :
I doubt that precept when a fan of ice
tremble perceptibly along the blue
and at the same time I remember twice
the accent on a single word which you
spoke to me once, but which, however nice
my instruments, I never may recapture
into phonation's prose or sober rapture

but merely point at what is never there
yet is that evanescent substance fleeting
as immaterial as beams in air
when televisions need those numbers greeting
them in their fixity, since these repair
(tip tip to digits, zipper's third heard meeting)
invisibly that grand array of stories,
the code of proxies for repealed stopped glories.

I am the forerunner of nothing : you
come from the desert, but await that flood
which drowns old Adam in its deepest blue
just at the same hour when I feel my blood
flow with its own devices, as if true
nature were nature by that grace whose food
holds it up every instant by the neck,
or lakes power cities by one stone-set check.

Adam reparadised : this second flesh
is almost infinitely calm, as though
I first returned now to my own express
thinking & walking, or as I might go
with perfect lightness where I repossess
life's long delights, and the descending snow
fall in mere silence to the pavement, where
it settles thickly, and the whitened air

fill with its flakes as April with shut buds.
It is impossible for me to keep
strong gestures of delight, withheld : your blood's
not part of nature merely, since its steep
trajectory redemptively dishudds
rain-soaked officiants, and their cares leap
up from their boxes, as I do from mine,
just when I see the night snow fall and shine

bringing third nature to each vent and drain
pinned in the tarmac. I look out across
the city which I start to see again
not as the palace of official loss
but as new light and glass whose clear refrain'
s collective self-correction, spars which cross
up to their apex where the frozen water
rests there at each triangulated quarter.

Lateness itself is obsolete : we start
at every moment, and by recollections
summon at each breath that antiquest part
wedged in our throats, & with whose misdirections
I cannot miss my way. The slowing heart
pulses its history of imperfections
into this novum; the most ancient thought
thinks me this instant to its first report.

This long expulsion of the tree of knowledge
thriving inside my lung, coughs bits,
fragments of certainty, each unacknowledged
presumption of known competence which sits
killing me slowly like a flawless solid :
each loud pertussion which stumps up & spits,
more painful than the last, the stubborn rest
labouring obdurately unconfessed

against relief, like furballs or a bone
stuck in the exit. Every breath I take
rasps at the passage of your grace : this drone
clasps at my windpipe, rattles when I shake
from top to bottom, perfectly alone
and perfectly unable to unmake
what settles in the hollows of my chest.
It ramifies with vegetable zest

just to be done with, as its bony branches
construct a universal skeleton;
it is a fossil calculus of chances,
proper to strangulate. I must go on;
my club feet buckle at the toe-stub dances;
each line's a tapeworm I must pull out from
the meaningless interior; I tread
step by step backwards, and the grieving dead

recede immeasurably from my sight.
I must make progress, but the forward march
runs in its sleep as on the spot all night
I am sunk downward where the spirits parch
my very throat up, and the rumoured light
reveals itself as fabulous, the arch
of explication and of wishful thinking,
the opposite of eating or of drinking.

Final aridity, may quick immersion
dispel mistrust, and this incarceration
inside derision : light drops, your aspersion
greet my dry forehead as a dispensation
able to turn each journey, since conversion
must redirect me, and your irrigation
turn just those arteries which fur and harden
to life's high desert or the dying garden.

Soft; stop now, stop; slow down; there is no need
to walk another step. Soon in my sleep
dim in-ear antiphons commence : blind greed
works efficacious providences; deep
screens of pleased leisure let the slow tropes bleed
down through the cochlea, as I would keep
unconscious instants to enjoy them twice,
or from the first reside in fatal ice.

As buds might settle in a tender shell
these instruments are sewn into my hearing :
I must have music, so the sand sings well
phantasmal ditties; from a spirit clearing
tracks none may tread must shuttle when a bell
alerts its icon, and I rest, unfearing,
while the lit packet burns down in my head.
The ring of messengers around my bed

lifts their bright buttons, so the real air
may not come near me : I shall sleep forever,
so dreams the cable when its port just there
clips into place, nor may one now dissever
z from sweet z because the sugared air
may not be eaten, and its fuels may never
self-interrupt nor think to disconnect
that apparatus none must once inflect

once with a variant, because all must
blink their identities, & welcome quick
reciprocation of the proper dust
known at each terminal, as tongue can lick
each pleasure-centre when an abstract lust
self-intercepts to make itself be sick
& vomit banquets for the peer review
of what I ate last Wednesday, or what you

would ingest intravenously. I drop;
my eyelids creep together, and I see
just through exhausted lashes one small drop
of grey, or pink, or pink-grey; it might be
an aircraft, or a satellite; the top
of my dim window, just now, lets me see
one intermittent, yet undoubted ray.
I can sleep, now; soon, now; here comes the day.

As the first note upon the cor anglais
summons the rustle of the winds to hold
a single note, because its speaking A
gathers the others to a chosen gold
standard of tuning, and they fall away
from their first anarchy of noise to told
metres and rhythms, and their rough cartoon
end in the disappointments of a tune

so that the oboe and the clarinet
are ringed and tethered, and the melting viol
must crystallize into the tone just set
& the rebec is checked, the base slips while
an equal temperament comes to fret
at each harmonic and an erstwhile vile
mathesis wrestles every little sound
into grand masterpieces which are found

each Saturday at 7.45;
or when I try to get to sleep, but think
a misplaced notion triggering a live
fear or excitement or a thought of drink
into my head, then I cannot contrive
not to twitch ceaselessly; my eyelids blink
and eyeballs blossom into arabesques
of greens and yellows like the red grotesques

conjured by thumbs into the sleepless jelly
of infinite conjecture, so the heart
clatters awake because the bloody telly
has been left on again, and with a start
I sit bolt upright as a line by Shelley
traverses consciousness, as though its art
were itself substance of this brain made sand
only to be erased upon the strand,

all possibility of rest recedes
into the night, and I am quite awake,
tied to the image of a line which speeds
from thought to thought as though its speech might make
some efficacious image, words to deeds,
or tunes to liturgies; so does day break;
so does each little splinter in the black
insinuate a colour into lack.

When, after amputations, anaesthetic
begins to wear off, and one point of pain
signals the places where a blank prosthetic
stands for a lost limb, and I feel again
its whole jammed motor, like the real aesthetic
thinking and feeling and knowing in the same
wild start of loss, so that the phantom hand
sketches, in air, own absence, & the grand

struck repertoire of gesture disappears,
stopped at the lopped wrist, so one pink informs
me that this night-hymn founders, since day clears
dark concentration to these public forms
set in the square. Wherever there appears
each green, cerise, or yellow, day's new norms
transvalue valuations with their gift
of unexhausted light; night's needful thrift

may be relaxed now, since the prodigal,
the sinking fund, the fire, the lavish sun
pours on the cool world all its power and all
its unsurpassed provision, as though one
at least should care for us, and for us all
dispense incessantly without return
his full insuperable wealth of light
waking up colours from the sleepy night

or somnolescent creatures from their beds.
Just as a poet, who had long resigned
himself to prose, can find some certain reds,
in popes or poppies, redirect the mind
to think in cadence, or the worst of heads
may be illuminated from its blind
sequence of habits, so this little tear
right at the corner of the night may bear

a new song, new life, or a new disaster :
the most melodious magenta brings
sense to its inner sense, since each sinks faster
to ineradicable sentience which sings
invisibly inside each still unmastered
radical datum, like a fact which sings
all day and night in the tormented head,
the unappeased exertions of the dead.

There is one moment in the waking day
which cannot be accounted for : as when
some spiritual fact, in what I say,
falls out, unspoken, from the net, it then
is as though disestablished, since I pay
no more regard to it than to some ten
bursts of lung-musculature which sustain
each floating thought, and in the summer rain

I may stroll absently around the lake.
So some component of arriving dawn
must still elude me, just because I make
my brain's best exit from the night, self-torn
from these privations when the dark I take
for an asylum or a cell is born
into this ruin of unceasing night.
I hardly can believe my eyes : the light

aches at my retina, and so some slip
of indigo or crimson disappears
from my false consciousness; one errant pip
drops to some bed in which there are no fears
to tend and water it; my eye must dip,
bearing the pressure of unfailing years
on the frail eyelid, which the sun can warm
just as it shields the iris from each form

which rings the bright horizon. I get up.
I walk back over to the bed; the sun
still in a dark room at the shaded mirror
begins to speak, and in the glass there one
corner or orange is at last lit up
and paints its sector with the slightest glimmer
repeated in the sink and then the cup
as each begins to chatter and to shimmer

with day's known talk, the deeper sleep of reasons.
I fall asleep into the instruments
of waking purpose and pretended freedoms.
I dream that fact which never once relents
obliterations of the times and seasons.
It is an hour which never once repents
its charmless bible of approved ejections,
strict scripture of compulsory dejections.

Better to fall asleep for real, the clock
complete its circuit of unhappy lapses :
the jobless spirit only may unlock
a proper melody of these relapses,
the foot without a mediating sock
tread out these measures till their best collapses
and I fall back to a forbidden bed
as though it were a meeting with the dead.

I hear the stream of traffic in the street.
The voice of homeless waters from afar
could not so stertorously roll : the bleat
of cancelled flocks inside an avatar
pleads through its onset, and my own prose feet
itch to walk out now, since these noises are
an audible resemblance of the air
sent through the window to my empty chair

where I abandon to itself the real
echolocation of the bricks and stones
sound bounces back from, as each rubber wheel
grips and caresses earth before it loans
its waterfall of decibels to reel
up and across to me, and whose sent drones
rise like the music of disowned worked labour,
the very tune which neighbour owes to neighbour.

I cannot not be thinking of the spring.
I live still, and the stench of rubbish floats
up to me here now as the sweetest thing
disintegrating vegetable notes
into its full reek, as a smell might bring
my wrapped face naked. As a fleet of boats
seen from a promontory may set sail
by one and one so that they almost fail

to be collected, yet begin to cleave
closely together as they breast the ocean
or single strands into a flag whose weave
incorporates each silk, so this emotion
is all at once the substance I believe,
the unidentifiable, life's notion :
surmise attends surmise, as thought to thought,
careless of every limit which they ought

to self-preserve inside, embarks and races
to known conjectures of the real : I
am not deleted, nor am merely traces
hidden in some part of the distant sky
but am instead that real life which faces
real breaths and eddies of the wind when I
walk down the street and hear the working traffic
burn and dissolve itself like the seraphic

instant of life, a still retained sublime.
Every last person must at last remove
his mask of signals, and the flow of time
freeze for an instant, since what still must move
still must be still until the force of rhyme
repel its name into the air : I love
whichever syllables I may not junk
but which fly upwards from a thought which sunk

into the train of represented phantoms.
All fail, all founder, all revert to air :
yet each flees singularly in unrandom
fury of disappearance, so that there
is nothing lost there but the fancied ransom
thought pays to thought whenever I would stare
fixatedly into this final night.
The snow falls heavily. The breaking light

revels and stalls in what it would reveal
in street and temple, and at last those sounds
which inside me have kept their ceaseless squeal
settle and drop to earth; speech beats its bounds,
working its line away from what I feel
into this silent print. My look rebounds
from each immaculate extent of white
no longer hidden in the modest night.

The shining surfaces of walls and spires
forgo distinction, as their equal blanks
return responses from the semi-choirs
of plinth and pediment : each rings its thanks
in uniformity of milk : free lyres
make themselves new again; the candid ranks
of roofs, doors, pavements, buses, trains and cars
await day's stern dismissal of the stars :

the street lights flicker off; the snow descends
thicker and thicker as the morning grows
into its first height, and the sky still sends
flake after flake into the light which throws
rainbows of rainbows at whose vanished ends
nothing is found except the fallen snow's
implacable inexorable white.
Farewell, farewell to darkness and to night.

I close the window, turn back to the chair.
Be still, old voices; let diurnal prose
bring the rejected detail; now let prayer
lie silent for a while, and day disclose
whatever happens really to be there
when the negated or the banished rose
may not be known, and its conjectured flower
should disappear into a leafless hour.

Not every mediation can be held
together at all moments; not each wound
kept open always. Speech must be repelled
from every surface where it would too soon
seize on its opposite. I am propelled
up from my chair, and from this sounding room.
I close the door now, and my tuneless feet
go down the stairs and out into the street.

Earlier versions of a small section of this poem were published at *Critical Documents* (www.plantarchy.us) and in *Eighteen Poems* (London: Eyewear, 2013). My thanks to Justin Katko and Todd Swift.